D1500650

MIRACLE OF
EFFORT

MIRACLE OF
EFFORT

THALIA'S AUTISM JOURNEY

JOHN A. FORTUNATO, Ph. D.

ARCHWAY
PUBLISHING

Copyright © 2023 John A. Fortunato, Ph. D.

All rights reserved. No part of this book may be used or reproduced by any means, graphic, electronic, or mechanical, including photocopying, recording, taping or by any information storage retrieval system without the written permission of the author except in the case of brief quotations embodied in critical articles and reviews.

This book is a work of non-fiction. Unless otherwise noted, the author and the publisher make no explicit guarantees as to the accuracy of the information contained in this book and in some cases, names of people and places have been altered to protect their privacy.

Archway Publishing books may be ordered through booksellers or by contacting:

Archway Publishing
1663 Liberty Drive
Bloomington, IN 47403
www.archwaypublishing.com
844-669-3957

Because of the dynamic nature of the Internet, any web addresses or links contained in this book may have changed since publication and may no longer be valid. The views expressed in this work are solely those of the author and do not necessarily reflect the views of the publisher, and the publisher hereby disclaims any responsibility for them.

Any people depicted in stock imagery provided by Getty Images are models, and such images are being used for illustrative purposes only. Certain stock imagery © Getty Images.

ISBN: 978-1-6657-4223-8 (sc)
ISBN: 978-1-6657-4225-2 (hc)
ISBN: 978-1-6657-4224-5 (e)

Library of Congress Control Number: 2023906643

Printed in the United States of America.

Archway Publishing rev. date: 06/01/2023

PREFACE

THALIA SAID TO A SCHOOL DISTRICT PSYCHOLOGIST IN eighth grade that she sometimes felt that the teachers, "don't get how hard it is for me." This was the latest of many emotionally-charged moments for Thalia in trying to overcome her autism spectrum disorder. Thalia understood that there were going to be occasions when dealing with her disability would be difficult. So much had already been asked of her. Thalia started intense schooling before she was three years old when the outcome of her journey was far from certain. Thalia learned that hard work, courage, and determination to achieve were necessary for her to navigate the education and social challenges that she was facing. Thalia demonstrated these personal characteristics throughout high school and college. She continues to display them in her career as an elementary school teacher. Thalia knows the daily effort that it takes to manage her life-long condition.

Thalia needed the dedicated support of her parents, Donnie

and Lorena. They were confronted with a traumatic reality that required perspective and patience, while fighting through their moments of sadness. Donnie and Lorena were determined to be part of the solution for their daughter. Family is at the center of Thalia's journey as it is Donnie's cousin, Lisa, who first noticed Thalia's autistic behavior symptoms and delivered her initial learning therapy sessions.

Each child diagnosed on the autism spectrum will have a different experience with the disorder. The following is Thalia's unique autism journey. There are some similarities between what Thalia and other children with autism and their families have to endure. Through Thalia's journey, this book aspires to offer insight into the experiences, the emotions, the challenges confronted, the sacrifices demanded, and the decisions needed to be made at different stages of a child's life.

Thalia's message to other children struggling with autism spectrum disorder and their families is that they are not alone. They are part of a community in which there are stories that can be shared that can help them on their journey. Thalia says, "an autism diagnosis does not mean a child cannot succeed. It just means that child will see the world in a different light." Thalia's simple hope in telling of her journey is, "to inspire autistic individuals to live up to their full potential and provide optimism to families."

CHAPTER 1

LISA WOKE UP IN THE MORNING LOOKING FORWARD TO HER grandmother, Maria's, seventy-seventh birthday party later that afternoon. It was a couple of days after Christmas and Lisa was very much in a festive mood. Four generations of the Morsillo family gathered on this late December day in 1999. Lisa was especially excited to see her cousin Donnie's daughter, Thalia, and her cousin Janet's daughter, Deanna. Thalia was born on August 20, 1997. Deanna was born thirty-nine days earlier, on July 12.

It had been a few months since Lisa saw Thalia and Deanna. Lisa had fun playing with them and she loved watching her youngest cousins interact with each other. Lisa was entertained by Thalia's ability to speak in both English and Spanish. Donnie's wife, Lorena, was born in Barranquilla, Colombia. Lorena's family moved to the United States when she was three years old. Lorena was teaching Thalia how to say different words in Spanish. Lisa would ask Thalia to, "say shoe in Spanish," with Thalia being able

1

to effortlessly reply, "zapato." They would laugh every time Thalia showed off her talent. Lisa expected this family party to be another day of similar enjoyment with Thalia.

The day suddenly turned out to be vastly different than Lisa imagined. Lisa immediately noticed that Thalia was acting in a way that was not typical of how she normally behaved. Thalia was not paying any attention to Deanna. It was as if Thalia did not know who Deanna was. Thalia was not talking or interacting with anyone at the party. Thalia was not responding when someone called her name. She did not even turn her head to look at the person who was trying to get her attention. Thalia often had a blank look on her face. She was in her own world.

Lisa was startled and concerned. She became fixated on watching Thalia's behavior. Lisa saw Thalia uncontrollably running around the restaurant where the party was held. Lisa observed Thalia repeatedly climbing onto a chair near a window where she would quickly and fiercely open and close the blinds. Thalia ran up to a table where people were sitting and she recklessly reached into a water glass to grab an ice cube. Thalia had no care about the consequences of breaking the glass and cutting herself or spilling water on the people as they sat at the table. Thalia then took off and resumed running around the restaurant.

Lorena spent most of the party chasing her daughter. Thalia ignored her mother's pleas to slow down or to come sit with her. Lorena got increasingly frightened as Thalia kept going near the top of the long staircase at the restaurant. Lorena continuously had to rush over to ensure that Thalia did not tumble down the stairs. Lorena had to raise her voice at one point to get the attention of some of the family members who were closer to the stairs so that they could catch Thalia before she might have fallen.

Lisa witnessed a tired and deflated look on Lorena's face. Lisa saw a mother who had no explanation for her daughter's behavior and who was working much harder than expected to calm her child. Lisa thought Lorena might have assumed that this is what it is like to raise a two-and-a-half-year-old child. Lisa felt that Lorena simply did not know that it should not be this difficult.

Others at the party were seemingly not aware of Thalia's alarming behavior. They probably thought that Thalia was just a rambunctious or excited child if they found the way that she was acting to be peculiar. Lisa, however, understood that Thalia's behavior was an indication of a problem for a child that age. Lisa believed that Thalia should have been playing with Deanna who was the same age and was someone with whom Thalia was familiar. Thalia ignoring her cousin was a huge cause of concern for Lisa. Thalia constantly running around the restaurant independently was another red-flag behavior. Lisa also thought that Thalia should have been aware of the potential danger of falling down a long staircase or carelessly reaching into a glass. Thalia had no fear.

Everything about the day was quickly becoming very emotional for Lisa. Her initial shock turned into a ferocious anxiety. Lisa was having difficulty processing what she was witnessing. She struggled to get clarity of her thoughts. Her mind was racing. She kept repeating to herself, "what is happening to Thalia?" Lisa could not completely focus on anything else that was occurring at the party. Lisa was consumed with fear of what her young cousin might be suffering from.

Lisa had a great curiosity about Thalia's situation, but she was conflicted at that moment about whether to approach Donnie and Lorena to get the answers to the many questions that were ravaging her brain. Lisa did not think that bluntly talking to them about Thalia's behavior was an option, especially at her grandmother's birthday party. Lisa could have asked Donnie and Lorena some benign questions, such as "is Thalia always this excited?" Or, "does Thalia get to play with other children?" Lisa ultimately felt overwhelmed that she did not initiate a conversation with Donnie and Lorena regarding Thalia's behavior.

Lisa could not bring herself to ask her siblings, John and Tricia, or her boyfriend, Rich, if they noticed anything unusual about how Thalia was acting. Lisa's observations would have to be the sufficient tool for which her suspicions about Thalia were raised. Lisa watched a scene the entire afternoon that was painfully obvious to her, but that nobody else was seeing. Lisa could have easily been brought to tears if she allowed herself.

Lisa maintained her composure so that the other family members at the party had no idea what she was thinking. It was her singular burden to deal with at this time. Lisa was emotionally drained and absolutely sick to her stomach by the end of the party. Lisa concealed her true feelings one final time when saying goodbye to Donnie, Lorena, and Thalia. She wondered if she might be wrong, but there were way too many signs. Lisa knew that a daunting path was ahead for them if what she suspected about Thalia was true.

CHAPTER 2

Lisa graduated from Bloomfield High School in New Jersey in 1990. She enrolled at Farleigh Dickinson University in Florham Park as a psychology major. An academic advisor at the university questioned Lisa as to what she was planning to do with a psychology degree. Lisa did not have a satisfactory response for her advisor, or herself, as to why she was pursuing psychology. A desire to help people in some capacity was certainly one reason, although Lisa was unsure how a psychology degree translated into an everyday job that she would find fulfilling. The academic advisor proposed to Lisa that she also get a teaching certification for general education and special education. Lisa was not overly enthused with the suggestion. She did understand the advisor's point about thinking of her long-term career. Lisa followed the advisor's recommendation.

Lisa completed the student teaching requirement for both education certifications. She did her general education and special education student teaching in a second grade classroom. Lisa did not enjoy either of her student teaching experiences. She did not feel a great passion for working in those classroom environments. Lisa was set to graduate with a psychology degree and her education certifications, but she could not envision any of those areas as her career. Lisa had not yet applied for a general education or a special education teaching position.

Lisa was working part-time at a computer lab on campus in her last semester of college, still contemplating her future. Lisa expressed frustration about her career options to her friend, Stephanie, who was also working part-time at the computer lab. Stephanie began to tell Lisa about the school where she was working that specialized in teaching children with severe learning and behavior disabilities, the Developmental Learning Center (DLC). Stephanie encouraged Lisa to visit the DLC. Stephanie was almost certain that there would be an opening for a teacher's aide position in the summer. Lisa's special education teaching certification met the qualification for the job. Lisa decided to apply. An interview at the school was arranged after Stephanie informed her supervisors and recommended Lisa.

Lisa arrived at her interview at the DLC with an open mind. She was to meet with some of the teachers and the administrative staff. She was going to observe the children in both one-on-one and group teaching settings. Lisa witnessed behaviors by the children that were beyond her imagination, even after being told by Stephanie about what she might see. The description by Stephanie could not capture this environment.

Lisa was told, and it was easy for her to notice, that some of the children had limited communication skills. Some children were saying only a few words or phrases. Other children were repeating their language or mimicking what was said to them by others.

Another child was screaming when communicating. Several children barely spoke at all. These children would point to what they wanted. Some children exhibited more aggressive behaviors. They might hit or pull the hair of a staff member or another student. Children might engage in self-injurious behavior, such as biting their hands. Some of the children in their teens possessed physical strength that required multiple staff members to help prompt and redirect these children to more appropriate behaviors.

It was an exhausting and emotional day for Lisa. She had a tremendous amount of sorrow and compassion for these children. Lisa also immediately felt an adrenaline rush as she was in this classroom setting. She loved it. Lisa was attracted to the intensity that she would have to bring every day if she worked at this type of school. She wanted the challenge of trying to help these children. Lisa believed that she could control her emotions and that she possessed the personality characteristics of patience, caring, and determination that were needed to perform well in this job. Lisa did not hesitate in accepting a position as a teacher's aide starting in the summer after she graduated college.

It was at the DLC that Lisa was introduced to the field of autism. Lisa had not heard the word, autism, at any point in her college education. Autism is a developmental spectrum disorder so each child will have a different experience with the disability. There are certainly notable differences in severity. There are some common characteristics of the disorder related to communication, social, and emotional deficiencies. Children with autism have language skills that are not developed at an age-appropriate level. They might not display any facial expressions. There is an absence of interest in peers. Children lose their ability to effectively play with others when they do not possess the appropriate communication and social skills. These children may retreat from these interactions. They, instead, engage in repetitive self-stimulating behaviors, such as independently running around, arm flapping, or developing a fixation on their own hands.

Children with autism desire structure. The slightest change to a child's routine can cause extreme anxiety and a tantrum. A child may have to take the same route going from place to place, eat the same food every day, or consistently line up toys in a certain way. Some children have an intense interest in a singular topic or object that it is hard for them to pay attention to any other subject. Other children have hypersensitivity to loud sounds. A visual fascination with lights or movement is another common sensory symptom that children with autism display.

These developmental deficiencies and behavior characteristics impede learning. Children with autism have difficulty maintaining their focus and following basic directions. Their mind does not permit them to comfortably and calmly work through an educational task or a social situation. The level of assistance that individuals on the autism spectrum require can range from one of constant care in their daily lives, to some who need minimal prompting and direction to achieve age-appropriate behaviors.

It was generally only those children who exhibited the most severe learning and behavior disorder characteristics that received an autism diagnosis at the time that Lisa started working at the DLC. Lisa was placed as a teacher's aide in a classroom that was led by an experienced teacher, Denise. Lisa learned so much from Denise. She felt that working with Denise instantly, and by far, surpassed both of her student teaching experiences. Denise quickly became a trusted mentor and friend to Lisa.

As the teacher, Denise was responsible for observing the individual skills that the children possessed and those that they were lacking once they arrived at the school. Denise then used that knowledge to develop the learning programs for each child in her class. Lisa was trained how to teach the learning programs, with Denise providing oversight and support. Lisa worked with a child in focused, one-on-one therapy sessions every day for many hours.

Lisa immediately gained great personal satisfaction from working at the DLC. She was becoming more convinced that teaching children with autism was going to be her career. She had a passion for helping these children. Lisa loved that she was making a difference in their lives. She felt a gratifying sense of purpose. A calling.

Denise was promoted to the role of supervisor as the summer that Lisa spent as a teacher's aide was ending. Lisa was asked to be the teacher for that class. Lisa was excited about the opportunity. She immediately accepted the job. Her career path was decided.

Lisa was working in a career that she never thought of growing up, or even during college. What Lisa learned in five years at the DLC enabled her to instantly recognize the prominent symptomatic behaviors for autism that she watched Thalia display. Every behavior that Lisa observed Thalia doing pointed toward an autism symptom. It was the behavior characteristics of poor communication skills, no situational awareness, showing no interest in others, and the fixation on objects that were all troubling. Lisa was able to understand that Thalia's acts of self-stimulation replaced her desire, or her need, to interact with the other people at the party.

Lisa came to learn the importance of early intervention and beginning to conduct education and behavior therapy with a child at a young age through her time at the DLC. Children who were as young as three years old attended the school. It was firmly believed that it was best for a child to start therapy as soon as possible once diagnosed with an autism spectrum disorder. Lisa witnessed positive behavior outcomes for many of the children who started therapy at an earlier age. Lisa strongly believed that there was a problem with Thalia and that it needed to be addressed, immediately. Lisa felt that a delay in Thalia receiving therapy could have devastating, life-altering consequences and greatly hinder her development.

All that Lisa learned, her abilities, and her experiences were being tested and called upon in the most meaningful way possible, a situation involving a family member. Lisa was still faced with another challenge. Lisa had to figure out how to tell Donnie and Lorena, as well as her Uncle Dan and Aunt Barbara, that their daughter, and granddaughter, had a learning and behavioral developmental disorder and was a child who needed to be evaluated for autism.

CHAPTER 3

WHILE LISA MADE IT THROUGH HER GRANDMOTHER'S party without mentioning her thoughts about Thalia to anyone, keeping those feelings all to herself was bothering her. Lisa could no longer contain her silence. Lisa blurted out, "I think Thalia has autism" on the car ride home with her parents, Artie and Vera, and Rich. The others in the car were stunned. Vera exclaimed, "oh, Lisa, what are you talking about? Don't say that!" The instant reactions were of understandable worry and unease. Vera said that she did not notice anything regarding Thalia's behavior that appeared strange. Lisa started to describe what she saw and, more importantly, what she thought that it meant. Lisa explained that all of Thalia's behaviors were alarming symptoms common in children diagnosed with autism.

Lisa felt relieved to talk about her concerns and fears. She could now discuss her observations with others, rather than having them repeatedly playing only in her mind. The announcement by Lisa about Thalia was difficult for Artie and Vera to hear and process. To some degree, a burden was placed on them as well by Lisa sharing this information. However, asking Lisa to be the sole person having to confront this problem would not have been fair. It also would not have been long before Lisa's family and Rich realized that something was seriously irritating her. Lisa was able to hide her emotions during her grandmother's birthday party, but that was for a limited period of a few hours.

Vera was nervous about how the other family members would react. Artie had a wonderful relationship with his older brother, Dan. Vera and Barbara were also very friendly. Artie, Vera, and Lisa did not want to upset their loved ones in any way. Vera was trying to think through how to approach this delicate issue. It was difficult envisioning how the conversation explaining the situation would unfold.

There was no immediate family gathering where they were going to see Donnie and Lorena. The next opportunity that Lisa could observe Thalia and further confirm her suspicions was unknown. Vera mentioned that Easter might be the next time that they would all be together. Lisa was emphatic that she did not want to wait that long before letting her thoughts be known.

Lisa understood the potential rift that she would cause and the possible angry, perhaps, unforgivable reaction that she would face if she was wrong. Lisa knew that tossing around a word as potent as autism could be irresponsible unless she was one hundred percent certain. The general public did not know much about autism. There was a stigma attached. Autism had connotations of severity, being irreversible, and being irreparable. Lisa had no idea what level of knowledge Donnie and Lorena had about autism. Lisa's parents, her brother, sister, and Rich were alarmed when Lisa mentioned that she believed Thalia had autism. They did not doubt Lisa, but there was no way for them to understand the gravity of the problem as Lisa. They could all just clearly see that Lisa was extremely concerned.

Lisa's conflict then became one of having moments where she began questioning herself. Lisa was basing everything on one observation. She thought, maybe, that the way that Thalia acted at the party was not how she typically behaved. Lisa wondered if she might be overreacting.

Lisa needed some reassurance. She talked to Denise and her colleagues at the DLC when she returned to work after the Christmas break. Lisa meticulously described Thalia's behavior. Denise and the others confirmed Lisa's suspicion. Denise offered to go with Lisa to do an observation of Thalia if that opportunity ever presented itself. Lisa was comforted by the support that she received from her DLC colleagues. They recognized how difficult the prospect of a family member being on the autism spectrum was for Lisa.

The corroboration of Lisa's initial assessment of Thalia from her colleagues gave her the needed confidence to discuss the situation with Donnie and Lorena when that time would eventually occur. Lisa knew that she had to come forward and reveal her thoughts at some point. Lisa was still contemplating the way for that conversation to transpire.

Lisa, John, and Tricia had close, friend-like relationships with Donnie and Janet, who were their older and only first cousins. Their families celebrated birthdays and most holidays together. The cousins spent many summer days with each other swimming at the community pool when they were kids. Lisa and Tricia were bridesmaids at Janet's wedding. John was Donnie's best man when he got married. As strong as these family bonds were, Lisa felt that unexpectedly calling Donnie and making this claim about his daughter seemed like overstepping.

CHAPTER 4

WHILE LISA WAS DEALING WITH HOW TO GET DONNIE and Lorena's attention regarding Thalia's condition, she was not aware that they were already grappling with Thalia's behaviors that they were seeing. Donnie and Lorena were not oblivious that there was a problem. They too were puzzled by Thalia's actions.

Donnie and Lorena knew that there were delays in Thalia's language, especially compared to other children her age. Thalia would say only one word or short phrases, such as "I'm tired," or, "where's the doggie?" One of the other longest sentences that Thalia consistently said was, "oh dear, what a mess," which she heard on television.

Thalia was not verbalizing any of her wants and needs. Thalia pointed to what she wanted or she would take Lorena's hand and walk her over to the desired item. Thalia was also not responding to her name being called. Thalia had been able to react to basic verbal directions the previous summer, for example if Lorena said, "come here, Thalia."

Donnie and Lorena noticed that Thalia was not interacting with other children. She did not have back-and-forth conversations. Thalia was not engaging in shared, imaginative play typical of children that age. Thalia replaced playing with others with many acts of self-stimulation. Thalia would become fixated on her hand with her eyes staring at it in mesmerized amazement as she rotated it back and forth. Thalia would repeatedly bring her hand back and forth to her nose. Thalia constantly twirled around. She rocked from side to side while standing. She occasionally flapped her arms.

Thalia demonstrated inconsistent eye contact. She would not look at the person who was talking to her. Thalia, at times, had a blank, almost zombie-like look on her face. She would stare at nothing in particular. Lorena became frightened when this occurred. Lorena would desperately try to get Thalia's attention and engage with her by getting her to look at the pictures in a book or attempt to play a game.

Other unusual behaviors were happening. Donnie and Lorena heard Thalia giggle for no reason as if she was being tickled as she was lying in bed before falling asleep. Thalia was not playing with toys in the same manner as other children. Thalia rarely played with any of her dolls. When she did, she would pick up the doll and throw it, rather than hold it and demonstrate an emotional attachment. Thalia's attention span while playing was also limited.

Donnie and Lorena did not know the cause of Thalia's behavior, similar to other parents in this circumstance. Donnie and Lorena both heard of the term, autism, but it did not immediately occur to them that this might be Thalia's problem. They, however, did not have the knowledge of autism and its symptomatic behaviors to lead them to the conclusion that this was the affliction that was causing Thalia's behavior difficulties.

Parents of children diagnosed on the autism spectrum are in many instances having to initially confront their child's situation with limited knowledge of the disability. This can be especially problematic for parents as they try to learn about their child's predicament while conflicting information about the causes and treatments of autism is being presented.

The overall number of children diagnosed with autism was dramatically increasing at the time that Thalia was first showing her alarming symptoms. One reason for the higher number of cases put forth in the news media was a greater public awareness of getting children with behavior deficiencies evaluated. Another reason was an adjustment in how the disability was being diagnosed. There was a shift from only the most severe cases to a more encompassing definition of what constituted a child as being on the autism spectrum. There was a desire of some parents to have an autism diagnosis rendered to have a child be eligible to receive special education support services offered by the government.

There was much debate about the cause of autism. The general question centered on if autism was caused by genetic or environmental factors. Some studies reported in the media found that autistic children appeared to have parts of their brains underdeveloped. One of the environmental factors that became prominent was that autism was caused by the vaccines for children that contained the mercury preservative, thimerosal.

The connection between thimerosal and autism was promoted to such an extent that thousands of parents filed lawsuits and the United States Congress held multiple hearings on the subject. Some medical professionals claimed that the link between thimerosal and children with autism was almost certain. Multiple scientific studies, however, generally showed no credible evidence of a link between thimerosal and autism. The Centers for Disease Control, the Food and Drug Administration, the World Health Organization, and the American Academy of Pediatrics all dismissed thimerosal as a cause of autism.

Donnie and Lorena contemplated explanations that would offer them some reasoning for the behaviors that they were witnessing on an increasingly daily basis. They thought that Thalia might have a hearing problem. In addition to Thalia not responding to her name being called, she would get frightened and hold or cover her ears when she heard a loud noise, such as a car horn or a fire truck siren. Thalia would run to Lorena to be picked up and held or she would grab onto Lorena's leg when she heard a loud sound. Thalia's hearing tests showed no issues. Her hypersensitivity and adverse reaction to loud sounds was another symptomatic behavior for autism.

Donnie and Lorena thought that Thalia might be shy and that was why she was not interacting with other children. Thalia mostly kept to herself. Thalia was, at least, never aggressive with other children. Lorena even wondered if teaching Thalia how to speak in both English and Spanish was causing her to have difficulty processing language. Thalia was sleeping and eating well causing Donnie and Lorena not to think that she had a physical medical condition.

Donnie and Lorena were further confused when trying to find a reason that explained these emerging behaviors of concern because Thalia had been hitting all of the critical age-appropriate benchmarks for a child. Thalia was sitting up and crawling when expected. She started walking at around nine or ten months old. She said her first words at that same time. Donnie and Lorena could see how Thalia was acting in comparison to their same-aged niece, Deanna. Thalia and Deanna's behaviors were similar for their first two years. It was difficult for Donnie and Lorena to understand how Thalia who demonstrated certain behaviors, could lose those capabilities.

Others were noticing Thalia's changing behaviors as well. Lorena's parents, Orlando and Ubiltrudis, were among the first to think that there was a problem. They watched Thalia as Donnie and Lorena went to work. Lorena dropped Thalia off every morning and Orlando would warmly greet his granddaughter as she walked through the door. Thalia was always excited to see her grandfather. She energetically greeted him when she first arrived. Orlando and Ubiltrudis noticed that Thalia was now quiet when she was at their house. It seemed strange. Orlando and Ubiltrudis mentioned their concerns to Donnie and Lorena.

Lorena's younger sister, Uby, often heard Thalia count in both English and Spanish. Uby noticed that Thalia stopped counting and that she was speaking less. Uby would see Thalia gazing, with her mind seemingly distant from what was occurring around her. Uby took Thalia with her to the mall one day. Uby thought to treat her niece to McDonald's for lunch. Thalia could not communicate what she wanted to eat when they arrived at the restaurant. Uby called Lorena and explained what was happening. Lorena and Uby started to cry on the phone. Lorena felt helpless that she was not there to assist her daughter.

Donnie's sister, Janet, saw Thalia staring at her own hand. She thought that it was a little peculiar, but certainly not a sign of a serious learning and behavior disability. Janet thought that every child is just a little bit different. Janet saw Thalia play well with her daughter, Deanna, in the past. Janet was more of a mindset that Thalia might be going through some sort of a development phase and that it would not last.

Dan too did not believe that there was a major problem with Thalia. He witnessed his granddaughter participating in many activities that other children were doing. He saw Thalia display motor skills of running, jumping, and swimming. He did not know that having developed physical capabilities generally does not offer much insight into whether a child may be autistic. Poor gross motor skills that a child exhibits might be an indication of autism if they are in combination with some of the other more prominent symptomatic behaviors.

Thalia was achieving other age-appropriate behaviors. She assisted in dressing herself. She could use utensils. A child's deficiencies in both gross motor skills and fine motor skills of not being able to effectively make hand movements hinder an ability to play. For example, a child may not be able to hold a crayon, use scissors, or mold clay. Thalia was able to perform these common actions of play. Thalia's coordination skills also led some in the family to doubt that there was a serious issue.

Barbara often went to Donnie and Lorena's house on Saturday to spend time with Thalia. Barbara noticed that when she spoke to Thalia that her granddaughter would not make eye contact. Barbara caught Thalia looking at her own hand as well. Barbara observed that Thalia tended to stay away from other kids and that she preferred to keep to herself when she was playing at the park. Barbara never said anything to Donnie and Lorena about what she was witnessing. Lorena did once raise a concern to Barbara about how Thalia was acting. Barbara responded to Lorena with the thought that she was probably overreacting. Barbara did not want to panic Lorena.

Barbara casually mentioned to Vera during one of their many phone conversations that Thalia was having some behavior issues. Vera thought that this was the proper moment to speak about the situation. Vera replied to Barbara by saying that Lisa noticed some disturbing behaviors when seeing Thalia at the birthday party. Vera suggested to Barbara that her speaking with Lisa might be helpful. Vera added that Lisa would welcome the opportunity to talk to Donnie and Lorena, but that she did not know how to approach them on a subject this sensitive.

The seriousness of the problem was elevated for Barbara knowing that Lisa was aware and concerned about Thalia's behavior. Barbara decided to speak with Lisa. Barbara informed Lisa about Thalia's behaviors that she noticed. Barbara described that Thalia would run around a store and that it was hard to keep track of her. None of Barbara's comments were surprising to Lisa. Barbara told Lisa at the end of their conversation that she would try to get Lorena to call her.

Lorena again mentioned to Barbara that she was nervous about the way that Thalia was acting. Barbara did not diminish Lorena's concern this time now that she had a better understanding of the matter after her conversation with Lisa. Barbara said to Lorena that she should speak with Lisa. Barbara remarked that Lisa had experience in dealing with children who had special education needs. Lorena started to cry. Lorena also undoubtedly knew that something had to change for Thalia. Lisa's phone soon rang.

CHAPTER 5

LORENA AND LISA ALWAYS HAD A GOOD RELATIONSHIP. THEY enjoyed each other's company at family parties. They, however, did not have a relationship where just the two of them spent time together going to a movie, shopping, or meeting for coffee. Lisa did not know to expect a phone call from Lorena, although it was a moment that she hoped would occur.

When Lorena called, she quickly confronted Lisa by asking her, "do you think there is something wrong with my child?" Lisa remained calm. She felt pressure in wanting to offer exactly the right assessment of the situation and advice for what next steps should be taken. Lisa knew that it was an intense subject that they were discussing. It was now time for Lisa to display courage. Lisa owed Lorena, Donnie, and Thalia her devoted honesty. Lisa replied, "I am concerned about the things that I saw." At this moment, Lisa was willing to risk any anger or frustration that would come her way if she was wrong about Thalia. Lisa definitely welcomed being wrong or there being an alternate explanation. Lisa's experience was pointing her toward an almost certain outcome.

Lorena questioned Lisa about the possibility of Thalia having a serious condition. Lorena explained to Lisa that Thalia started nursery school a couple of months after her second birthday. The nursery school was located at Trinitas Hospital in Elizabeth, New Jersey, where Lorena worked as a physical therapist assistant. It was an ideal arrangement for Lorena to check on Thalia throughout the day. Lorena said to Lisa that she was friendly with the teachers at Thalia's nursery school. The teachers did not report any out-of-the-ordinary behaviors of the severity that Lisa was claiming. Lisa had a high degree of certainty that the nursery school teachers did not have the knowledge that would have led them to think that any peculiar behaviors by Thalia were symptoms of autism.

Lorena told Lisa that a pediatrician examined Thalia. Lorena wanted to convey to Lisa that she and Donnie were aware that Thalia was displaying some irregular behaviors and that they already took steps to address the problem. The pediatrician felt that there was nothing wrong with Thalia. The visit did not provide any specific answers as to the cause of Thalia's unusual behaviors. The pediatrician, instead, offered a sense that these behaviors could soon end. Lorena repeated the pediatrician's assessment to Lisa numerous times during their phone conversation.

Lisa tried to be understanding on this point, but she explained to Lorena that the pediatrician was not trained to properly diagnose Thalia's condition. Lisa experienced through her work at the DLC where a pediatrician missed diagnosing a child on the autism spectrum. Lisa explained to Lorena that it was a pediatric neurologist, a doctor specializing in evaluating these types of learning and behavior development disorders in children, who needed to conduct an assessment of Thalia.

Lorena asked Lisa directly, "do you think Thalia has autism?" Lisa felt that ethically she should not provide Lorena with an affirmative statement of Thalia's condition. Lisa did not have formal training in diagnosing. She was not a professional in that medical field. Her experience was in the treatment of children who were already diagnosed as being on the autism spectrum. Lisa viewed her responsibility was to recommend that a child be evaluated by the appropriate doctor who can offer the proper diagnosis. Lisa was confident in saying to Lorena that she saw enough of Thalia's behavior that she strongly believed that Thalia needed to be immediately evaluated.

Lisa arrived at a strategy during the phone call where her sole objective of the conversation was to convince Lorena to bring Thalia to a pediatric neurologist. Lisa was desperate in needing Lorena to trust her at this moment. Lisa said to Lorena that if Thalia was evaluated by a pediatric neurologist and if that medical professional said that there was not a problem, she would, "promise to drop the issue and never bring it up again." Lorena finally agreed.

Lorena then asked Lisa if she would come to the house and observe Thalia. Lisa gladly visited. Lisa had not seen Thalia since her grandmother's party. Lisa was curious to see how Thalia was now behaving a few weeks later. Lorena informed Lisa in greater detail about how Thalia was consistently acting. Lisa saw Thalia behave at the house in a way that confirmed her concerns. Lorena again asked Lisa if she thought that Thalia had autism. Lisa again responded that she could not offer a diagnosis. Lisa just continued to encourage Lorena to have Thalia evaluated by a pediatric neurologist. Lorena understood that making an appointment for Thalia to be examined was the next step. Lisa accomplished what she needed to in her conversations with Lorena. Lisa was relieved that they were starting on a path to getting real answers.

CHAPTER 6

THERE ARE OBVIOUSLY NOT AS MANY DOCTORS SPECIALIZING in pediatric neurology as there are fewer patients with this need in comparison to the medical conditions that affect larger segments of the population. It was becoming a challenge to schedule an appointment with a pediatric neurologist as more parents were seeking to have their child evaluated for autism. The possible delay in getting an appointment was another reason why Lisa was pushing for Lorena to quickly act.

After the conversations with Lisa and having an understanding that Thalia needed to be evaluated, Donnie and Lorena shifted their mindset. They would be proactive and no longer placid spectators in their daughter's journey. Lorena received referrals for multiple pediatric neurologists from Thalia's pediatrician. Lorena spent all of her time and energy fervently calling those doctors to get the earliest appointment possible. On April 10, 2000, Thalia was examined for autism for the first time.

There is no simple diagnostic procedure that detects autism, such as a blood test or a scan. A pediatric neurologist conducts an examination of a child's learning and behavioral development by asking questions of the parents and, if possible, the child, and by doing an observation of the child. The doctor assesses how the child responds to various communication prompts and opportunities for interaction.

Lorena filled out two autism screening forms before Thalia's appointment. Lorena's answers on one form indicated that Thalia had five of the twelve behavior features present for autism. Lorena's responses involved Thalia's language delays, a lack of social interaction with others, and her self-stimulating behaviors. Lorena wrote about Thalia's staring fixation on her hand and her repeatedly bringing her hand up to her face.

The other screening form that Lorena completed pointed to Thalia having five of the ten behavior features present for autism. These behavior features included Thalia not playing pretend games, not bringing things to her mother to show them to her, and not following simple directions. Lorena also described that Thalia was not interacting with other children. Lorena noted that Thalia did not show an interest in her six-month-old cousin, Janet's youngest daughter, Daria.

At the start of the examination, Lorena described in detail to the doctor Thalia's behaviors that she and Donnie were witnessing. Lorena highlighted Thalia's communication difficulties. She explained how Thalia developed language, but that she mostly stopped talking. Thalia's speaking now almost solely consisted of her repeating words and phrases. Lorena did mention to the doctor that Lisa also noticed Thalia's concerning behaviors, pointing out that Lisa was a relative who had experience as a teacher of children with autism.

The doctor began putting Thalia through an evaluation. He asked Thalia some basic questions, such as "what did you do today?" And, "where is the light?" Thalia did not respond. Thalia was not being overly cooperative during the examination. She could not follow the doctor's one-step instructions at an age-appropriate level. Thalia displayed inconsistent and fleeting eye contact with the doctor.

Lorena could see that Thalia was getting frustrated and that she did not want to be examined. Thalia began to cry, hard. Lorena felt her chest pounding as she watched her daughter. The nerves and fears that Lorena had walking into the doctor's office were dramatically increasing. Lorena began to get light-headed upon seeing how distressed Thalia was during the examination, almost to the point of passing out.

Thalia was left alone and merely observed during periods of the examination. Thalia was happier during these times. She was comfortably walking around the room and looking out of the window. She had a sense of calm. Being left alone was certainly preferable to continuing to be prodded by the doctor. The doctor after a lengthy examination offered a diagnosis of "Autism Spectrum Disorder – suspect this to be Pervasive Developmental Disorder."

It was an overwhelming day for Donnie and Lorena. The emotions were incalculable having received the most feared diagnosis. Lorena was devastated. There was profound sadness. Anger, anxiety, fear, and guilt were all present. Lorena questioned if she was a bad mother or if she did something wrong that caused Thalia to be this way. Lorena wondered if she would ever again hear her daughter call her, "mom." Lorena began to think that all of the dreams and aspirations that she had for Thalia were fleeting, if not unattainable. Lorena was completely dejected when thinking if Thalia would be able to make friends, attend college, or get married.

Donnie was stoic while at the doctor's office. He did not say much. Donnie grew frustrated as the doctor referred to the movie, *Rain Man*, an academy-award-winning movie that features the actor, Dustin Hoffman, playing a character with autistic behaviors. The doctor mentioned that at some point Thalia could have to be put in a special home. Perhaps, the doctor was offering worst-case scenarios in trying to help Donnie and Lorena adjust to a new reality. This cold and bleak approach was not what Donnie thought was needed at this time. Donnie felt that this type of pessimistic talk seemed premature. Donnie was not going to accept any of the life outcomes for Thalia that the doctor was describing as possible without first trying everything that could be done to help his daughter. Donnie felt a steely determination growing through his sadness.

Donnie became emotional when he got home and called his mother to tell her that Thalia was on the autism spectrum. Telling people is difficult. There is an unnecessary and unwarranted embarrassment associated with a diagnosis. It can feel almost insulting for the parents upon hearing a doctor say that there is something wrong with their child. It is when the parents are telling others that they may feel that they are being judged as the reason for their child having a disability. In reality, they and their child are victims of an insidious condition and an incredibly unfortunate situation.

All of the family members when speaking with Donnie and Lorena realized that they were overcome with fear. It was the upcoming period of the unknown that exacerbated everyone's tense emotions. Getting people to understand what an autism diagnosis means presented another obstacle. When Lorena told her father that Thalia had autism, he did not know what it was. He was simply heartbroken to hear that anything was wrong with his first granddaughter. Orlando's greatest concern was that Thalia's condition was irreversible. He asked Lorena what could be done. Lorena was uncertain of the correct answer at that point. Orlando told his daughter that he would help her in any way that he needed to, not knowing what that could be. His deep sorrow was equaled only by a feeling of helplessness.

Uby's immediate worry was that of the long-term effects. Uby tried to comfort her sister, seeing how completely devastated she was. Lorena told Uby of her desire to have Thalia once again call her, "mom." Uby was about to leave for college in a few months. It was an added obstacle for Uby knowing that she might not always be physically present to help her sister.

Janet was surprised when she was told that Thalia was diagnosed with autism. She did not believe that was her niece's condition. It did not seem right. To Janet, autism was an extreme worst-case scenario and a word reserved for children with the most severe behavior problems. Dan had a similar reaction. He was still in a bit of denial about his granddaughter.

It was not until Lisa explained to everyone in the family that certain behaviors of Thalia were the same as those displayed by children who were diagnosed with autism that they started to understand. Lisa educated them on how Thalia's acts of self-stimulation were a replacement for social interactions because she was not able to effectively communicate and develop her play skills. The family members started to pay greater attention to how Thalia acted now that they had more awareness. They better recognized the concerning behaviors and they were gaining a perspective of what those actions meant.

Lorena called Lisa and informed her of what the pediatric neurologist said. Lisa was not surprised at the diagnosis. It was exactly what she expected to hear. Lisa was prepared to offer her advice about how to proceed. There was no longer a debate for Lisa. The diagnosis meant that Thalia needed treatment. Lorena, however, quickly told Lisa that she wanted to get a second opinion. Lisa replied that she understood, especially knowing how devastating the news that Lorena was just given. Lisa then said to Lorena with some emphasis that, "the clock is ticking," and that she did not want to delay too long before Thalia started education and behavior therapy sessions.

Lisa knew that there had to be a balance when talking to Donnie and Lorena, as with speaking to all parents in this situation, between compassion and the harsh reality. Lisa was figuring out when she had to be more direct in discussing the problem with Donnie and Lorena, and the other times when she should show more empathy. Lisa understood that any reactions by Donnie and Lorena to the blunt advice that she might offer them were secondary to her saying what she felt was needed. The stakes for Thalia were simply too high.

CHAPTER 7

THALIA WAS EVALUATED BY A SECOND PEDIATRIC NEUROLO-
gist eleven days after her first appointment. Lorena again
described in detail all of Thalia's symptomatic behaviors at the
beginning of the examination. She stated to the doctor that Thalia,
"is not paying attention like other children." Lorena explained
Thalia's communication difficulties and her repeated self-stimulating behaviors. Lorena emphasized that Thalia constantly stared
at her own hand.

Lorena pointed out Thalia's positive behaviors. She informed
the doctor of Thalia's ability to recognize some letters and numbers.
She told the doctor that Thalia was able to complete six-to-ten-
piece puzzles and that she could name all of the Teletubbies, the
characters of a popular PBS children's television show. Lorena
described Thalia's coordination capabilities of her walking up and
down stairs in an alternating manner and that she started to pedal
a tricycle. Lorena mentioned to the doctor that Thalia could assist

in brushing her teeth and that she drank from a cup. Lorena was trying to highlight all of these behaviors that Thalia was doing to provide a more complete, optimistic picture. Perhaps, Lorena was doing this in the hope that this doctor would arrive at a favorable conclusion.

Thalia again cried during the examination. Thalia screamed in a high-pitched shrill as the doctor tried to evaluate her. Thalia was given a lollipop and a breakfast bar to hold. She became slightly calmer when holding these items in her hand. Thalia was not making sustained eye contact with either the doctor or Lorena. When Thalia did look at Lorena, it was for only a couple of seconds. The doctor witnessed Thalia repeatedly bringing the palm of her hand back and forth to her face. Thalia spent much of the visit in her stroller. She was often rocking forward and backward while in the stroller as the doctor tried to conduct the examination. Thalia became upset when Lorena tried to take her out of the stroller.

The second pediatric neurologist conducted similar assessments and received similar results as the first doctor. Thalia did not respond when the doctor asked her basic questions. Lorena tried to interact with Thalia by asking her, "where is your nose?" Thalia showed no interest in responding to her mother's question. Lorena then brought her face up close to Thalia's and asked her, "where is my nose?" Thalia raised her finger and touched Lorena's nose. When Lorena prompted Thalia, "to touch her ears," she reached out and touched her mother's earrings. This exercise did not last long and Thalia again became disinterested. Thalia did not respond when Lorena asked her, "where is mommy's pelo (hair in Spanish)?" The doctor requested that Lorena show Thalia a book of dolls. Thalia paid no attention to the book. She looked away from her mother.

The second pediatric neurologist arrived at the diagnosis of

"Pervasive Developmental Disorder with autistic features" at the conclusion of the examination. The doctor indicated that attending nursery school might show some socialization improvement through peer role modeling. The doctor, however, forcefully indicated that Thalia required specialized schooling. The doctor stated in the report detailing the evaluation that, "it is recommended that she be placed in a program that has therapists/teachers with expertise in autism."

This was the first formal documentation of Thalia receiving non-traditional schooling. It was difficult for Donnie and Lorena to hear, but reading this recommendation and it appearing on a printed page in black and white brought an additional level of emotional distress. It was the latest sober realization that the autism diagnosis was going to be included in Thalia's permanent medical record that would be used for school. Donnie and Lorena feared that this might impact how their daughter would be judged. They instinctively questioned, will people in school think less of Thalia? Will people think that Thalia cannot do something before giving her a chance?

Lorena called Lisa after the appointment with the second pediatric neurologist. The conversation was similar to the one that they had after Thalia's first pediatric neurologist visit. Lorena informing Lisa that Thalia received a diagnosis that placed her on the autism spectrum. Lisa trying to convey to Lorena the urgency of starting the process of getting Thalia therapy.

Lorena wanted yet another opinion. Lisa saw this in other parents as well where they were still not convinced of the diagnosis, or they were not ready to act on the diagnosis that was given. Many parents' uncertainty and fear about what is going to happen to their child lead to their hesitancy to act. Lisa had seen parents being an impediment to their child receiving the timely help that was needed. Lisa did not want that to be the case with Thalia where they missed the early intervention treatment window when the most significant education and behavior progress could occur.

An examination of Thalia by a third pediatric neurologist was conducted thirteen days after her second appointment. It was a similar experience to the other two doctors' evaluations. Thalia's language delay was obvious and was the cause of the greatest concern in the estimation of the third doctor. The result of the examination was again Thalia being diagnosed with an autism spectrum disorder.

This pediatric neurologist was more optimistic. The doctor explained that there was a favorable prognosis for improvement because Thalia developed some language. The doctor pointed to the fact that because Thalia spoke a few words and phrases automatically put her in a better position for positive long-term results. This characteristic was mentioned in the report of the first pediatric neurologist, but that respite of optimism was completely drowned out by that doctor's more dreadful potential outcomes. Donnie and Lorena were also trying to cope with hearing the autism diagnosis for the first time. There was less of a shock factor by the time of the third pediatric neurologist appointment. The autism diagnosis was expected. It was slightly easier for Donnie and Lorena to be more receptive and measured in listening to what this doctor was saying.

The third pediatric neurologist indicated that another positive for Thalia's long-term development was that she showed an interest in others in the past, despite her current level of social interaction and play skills not being age-appropriate. Often typical of children diagnosed on the autism spectrum, the long-term outlook would have been much more dire if there had not been any language or interest in others displayed.

The third pediatric neurologist was as clear as the other doctors in that Thalia's learning deficiencies needed to be immediately and comprehensively treated by trained professionals. Improvement was not going to magically occur. Thalia was not going to grow out of her condition. There was no surgical procedure or medication that would completely solve the problem. Thalia needed to learn how to communicate, process information, and socially and emotionally behave so that she could become more comfortable interacting with others.

The recommendation by each of the pediatric neurologists was for Thalia to be enrolled in an early intervention education program. It was stressed that Thalia needed a full-day, full-year program with intense speech and language therapy and occupational therapy that would help her further develop everyday life skills, coordination, and movement capabilities.

The autism diagnosis by the third pediatric neurologist affirmed a reality. There was no more guesswork about Thalia's condition. Acceptance of this reality and developing a plan for helping Thalia were now what confronted Donnie and Lorena. How they approached the situation would be a defining moment in the life of their daughter, and their lives. This was the time when Thalia needed them the most. Donnie and Lorena promised each other that they were going to be Thalia's voice and support system.

Donnie and Lorena knew that emotion could consume them to the point where it affected their behavior. It would have been easy for Donnie and Lorena to feel sorry for themselves, but those thoughts would not help Thalia. The moments of despair and sadness that would inevitably occur would have to be brief, with the focus quickly shifting to what was required to be done moving forward. Donnie and Lorena understood that they would be useless to Thalia and her progress if they were not functional.

Having perspective was important. Donnie and Lorena decided

that they would no longer question how and why this happened to Thalia. Dwelling on those questions of causality and trying to assign blame would be irresponsible and also of no help to Thalia. Donnie and Lorena had to be strong and logical. They were about to embark on many decisions regarding Thalia's learning and behavior development.

Donnie and Lorena agreed to rationally and calmly discuss decisions with one another. They were going to make decisions one step at a time. Donnie and Lorena understood the need to be patient and that the behavior change successes were not going to be instant, a point emphasized by Lisa. The improvements might be incremental, but collectively they would lead to the desired long-term outcome. Donnie and Lorena were prepared for whatever sacrifices they would have to make on Thalia's behalf. They were determined to be part of the solution. It was the exact temperament that the situation demanded, and their daughter needed.

CHAPTER 8

LISA HAD NOT HEARD FROM LORENA FOR A COUPLE OF WEEKS. She was getting increasingly nervous because of her deep belief that early intervention treatment was vital for Thalia's development. The call that Lisa desired finally occurred after Thalia's third pediatric neurologist appointment. Lorena began this phone conversation by asking Lisa, "what do we do?" Lorena was somber, but not defeated. She was aligned with the new reality of having the focus solely be on Thalia getting better. Lisa was relieved and, in some aspects, excited to hear that Donnie and Lorena were ready to move forward.

Lorena asked Lisa during their phone conversation if she would come observe Thalia at her nursery school. Lisa asked Denise from the DLC to attend this observation with her. Denise offered to accompany Lisa on an observation when Lisa first told her about Thalia's behavior. Denise readily agreed to Lisa's request. Lorena would not come with Lisa and Denise on the nursery school visit as they did not want Thalia to see her mother and spend the time being only by her side. Lisa and Denise wanted to see how Thalia naturally acted at nursery school.

The children were sitting with their legs crossed in a circle when Lisa and Denise arrived at Thalia's nursery school. Thalia, however, was standing and twirling around on her own. Thalia would twirl into the circle that was formed by the sitting children. Thalia acted as if she did not realize that the other children were present. Thalia also did not notice that Lisa was in the classroom. Lisa was someone whom Thalia should have recognized.

Lisa asked the nursery school teacher if this day was typical of how Thalia behaved. The teacher indicated that it was. For Lisa, the visit to Thalia's nursery school was another confirmation of everything that she first witnessed at her grandmother's birthday party a few months earlier. Lisa and Denise did not spend much time at the nursery school. A longer observation was not necessary. Both Lisa and Denise easily concluded that Thalia needed intensive education and behavior therapy.

Having an official diagnosis rendered by a doctor from a practical standpoint makes available special education support services provided by the state or the local school district. The Individuals with Disabilities Education Act of 1975 passed as a federal law guarantees that students with learning disabilities have a free, appropriate public education available in the least restrictive environment. The law ensures that children with disabilities receive the special education and related support services that are required to address their individual needs.

The states administer special education programs and services that fulfill the free, appropriate standard. The state government in New Jersey oversees programs for all children experiencing learning and behavior development delays until a child reaches the age of three. The local school district then assumes responsibility for a child's education. Early intervention services are provided if a child is determined to have a thirty-three percent behavior delay in one, or a twenty-five percent behavior delay in any two of the following areas: cognitive skills, communication skills, social/emotional or adaptive skills, and physical development skills, including motor skill delays or vision and hearing problems.

Representatives of the state of New Jersey evaluated Thalia on May 3 at her nursery school. Thalia was three months shy of her third birthday; thirty-three months old. The state evaluator assessed Thalia as age appropriate for her gross motor skills. Thalia showed that she was capable of running, jumping, hopping, and maintaining her balance with no difficulty. Thalia was found to be at a developmental level of twenty-two months for her fine motor skills, twenty-two to twenty-four months for her cognitive skills, and eighteen to twenty-four months for her adaptive or self-help skills.

Thalia was at a developmental level of twelve to fifteen months for her receptive communication skills. She had difficulty processing and understanding what was being said to her. Receptive communication comprehension requires a child's attention and concentration, problematic attributes for Thalia. Thalia was at the same twelve to fifteen-month level for her expressive communication skills, the messages that a child produces. Thalia's expressive communication deficiencies were exhibited by her inability to use words, speak in sentences, and offer non-verbal gestures that convey meaning. There was also a noted concern regarding Thalia's social and emotional behavior.

The outcome of the evaluation was that Thalia showed a twenty-five percent behavior delay in communication skills and adaptive play skills. Thalia met the state's criteria and was eligible for special education support services. The recommendation from the state evaluator was that, "Thalia would benefit from enrollment in developmental services with an emphasis on improving communication, social awareness, and interactive and play skills."

An Individualized Family Service Plan was created for Thalia. The documented desired outcomes for this plan were that Thalia will say her name and that she will be able to better follow basic directions. Thalia was offered by the state to receive special education instruction twice per week for one hour, and speech and language therapy once per month for one hour. The state services were planned to start in June and end in August when Thalia turned three years old. These services would temporarily fill in the time period before a more long-term plan would be developed by the local school district.

Lorena informed Lisa of the state's plan for Thalia. Lisa thought that this amount of therapy was not nearly enough. Lisa believed that it would have no or very little effect. Lisa felt strongly that Thalia needed education and behavior therapy every day for several hours, as she did with the children whom she worked with at the DLC. It was only a few months until Thalia's more permanent schooling would be arranged, but Lisa kept emphasizing that getting started immediately on comprehensive therapy sessions was critical. The time was precious and those months until September could not be wasted. Lisa was clear and firm in making these thoughts known to Donnie and Lorena.

Lisa proposed to Donnie and Lorena that she work with Thalia. Lisa pointed out that she would spend more hours with Thalia in a couple of days than the state was offering to spend over this period of months. Donnie and Lorena figured that more hours of therapy would benefit Thalia. They put their trust in Lisa. The services being offered by the state are the only option for some families.

Securing private services could be very expensive. Donnie and Lorena had a resource in Lisa that many others did not have.

Most relevant for any family once a child receives an autism spectrum diagnosis is learning the treatment options. As with trying to understand the causes of autism, sifting through the contradictory information about the available treatment options that are being discussed in the media or online can be confusing. It is overwhelming for parents who are trying to evaluate and decide which of the many treatment options that they are hearing about is the method that will get their child to best flourish.

Media reporting discussed a variety of methods that were being used to treat children with autism at the time that Thalia was diagnosed. Reports surfaced about the effectiveness of a medication used to treat obsessive-compulsive disorder, Clomipramine. Some parents tried putting their children on psychiatric medications, including antidepressants, stimulants, such as Ritalin, and antipsychotic drugs that were used to treat schizophrenia.

Alternate treatments were tried by parents who were desperate for a change in their child's behavior. Some parents paid to have their child go horseback riding, swim with dolphins, or receive healing touch therapy as part of their autism treatment. Other parents had their child undergo sensory integration techniques, where a therapist would use swings, a weighted vest, or a special brush gently gliding on a child's skin. A variety of dietary options or having a child take a large dose of vitamins were being used. Some parents resorted to their child receiving hormone injections. The scientific research generally did not support any of these treatments. Some of these methods might temporarily calm a child, but the underlying behaviors were not being treated or improved.

Lisa explained to Donnie and Lorena that she was going to use applied behavior analysis as the teaching method for Thalia.

Applied behavior analysis is used to teach the variety of communication and social behavior skills that affect children with autism. The core principles of applied behavior analysis are individualized learning programs that address a child's needed skills. It is important to make sure that what is being taught directly focuses on a child's specific behavior problems. The teaching might be delivered in a one teacher to one student format in the early stages of therapy. Teachers use positive reinforcement in the form of verbal praise and a child's desired items to motivate learning.

Applied behavior analysis provides the repetition and structure that a child with autistic symptoms needs to better learn. There is a careful collection of data to establish a child's skill level and determine when to advance a child to the next skill. Each child has a unique set of skills and progresses at a different pace. If a child needs more work in developing a particular skill, that is what is done. Progress is when a skill is learned, not by merely teaching a child something more advanced. This approach to learning requires a great amount of time.

Applied behavior analysis was the teaching method that Lisa became exposed to at the DLC. She witnessed firsthand how this approach was successful in improving the behavior of many children on the autism spectrum. Moreover, applied behavior analysis was the most scientifically supported method for the behavior improvement of children with autism. The United States Surgeon General in a 1999 report on mental health concluded that, "thirty years of research demonstrated the efficacy of applied behavioral methods in reducing inappropriate behavior and in increasing communication, learning and appropriate social behavior."

How the applied behavior analysis sessions are conducted is a vital element of success. The National Academy of Sciences issued a report in 2001 that detailed the effectiveness of applied behavior analysis if it is properly implemented. Research generally showed that applied behavior analysis produced and maintained the best outcomes when the following conditions were present: a child received therapy of at least twenty-five and sometimes forty hours per week, the instruction was done in a one-on-one setting, the treatments were started with a child as early as possible, the therapy lasted over a period of many years, and the therapy sessions were conducted by a qualified professional trained in teaching children with behavior disorders. The National Academy of Sciences report also found that parents being involved in their child's treatment was particularly helpful. As those researching applied behavior analysis document the successful improvement in the behavior of many children, they are clear in explaining that no treatment method offers guaranteed positive outcomes for all children diagnosed on the autism spectrum.

Lisa's extensive training and experience with applied behavior analysis gave her confidence that using this teaching method would help Thalia. Lisa somewhat began developing a plan in her mind for how to work with Thalia months ago, almost when she first observed her symptomatic behaviors. It now consumed much of her thoughts. If Lisa was feeling any pressure in helping Thalia, she knew that those emotions had to be secondary and overcome. Lisa was being relied upon to help her cousin.

CHAPTER 9

L ISA WAS TAKING A NEW JOB WITH THE CLINTON TOWNSHIP school district. She was hired to be a teacher in a special education classroom specifically for children with autism. It was the school district's first classroom that was designed to implement the applied behavior analysis teaching method. Lisa was thrilled to see a traditional elementary school using this approach. She was excited to run her own classroom using the techniques that she learned at the DLC. It seemed like the next logical step in her career.

Lisa was to start her job in September, making her available to work with Thalia throughout the summer. Lisa had the responsibility of developing learning programs for several students, as well as training new teacher's aides when she worked at the DLC. She would have a singular focus of working with Thalia for the summer months.

Lisa started therapy sessions with Thalia in late June. Lisa often brought Tricia with her. Donnie and Lorena already left for work when Lisa and Tricia arrived at the house on the first day. Lorena's father, Orlando, watched Thalia in the morning. Lisa first needed to establish an environment that would get Thalia to positively respond. Lisa wanted to foster a love of learning in Thalia and get her to enjoy doing the therapy sessions.

Orlando questioned if he should leave the house. He wanted to be there if Thalia needed him. Lisa suggested that it might be best for Thalia if he was not there. Lisa explained to Orlando that Thalia had to be focused if these learning sessions were going to achieve their desired results. Thalia could try to stay near Orlando if she knew that he was in the house. Orlando might have tried to stop the learning sessions if Thalia got upset and started to cry. A sympathetic grandfather could easily be convinced by his young granddaughter to hold her or do something that prevented her from having to partake in a therapy session. Lisa was not there to babysit or play with Thalia. Lisa needed Thalia to know that this was a time for learning, especially at the beginning of her treatment. Lisa persuaded Orlando that an environment with no distractions was how the learning needed to be done to help Thalia. Orlando understood and he left the house.

Lisa set up a workroom for herself and Thalia. Lisa had to learn the extent that Thalia would be able to focus during their therapy sessions. Lisa's initial step was to get Thalia to sit in a chair and stay attentive to what she was about to instruct her to do. Lisa knew that Thalia's disability made her prone to run around and do other self-stimulating behaviors. Lisa was prepared to gently prompt Thalia to sit in a chair if needed, an act that she had to do at the DLC with some of the children who had more severe disabilities.

Getting Thalia to sit down and listen to basic instructions was quickly achieved. Thalia sat in a small plastic chair typical for a child her age. Lisa sat across a table from Thalia in a similar type of chair so that she could be at eye level with her. Lisa sat on a side of the table to be even closer to Thalia at times.

Lisa could now focus on starting the educational aspects of the therapy sessions. Lisa began by working on Thalia's identification and recognition of objects. Lisa put out a set of pictures of different objects. It could be as few as three objects at the earliest stages of therapy depending on the child. Lisa told Thalia what each object was called. Communicating the name of the object started the process of Thalia learning how to say the name herself. The long-term objective was for her to use the word to request that object. Lisa would then prompt Thalia to identify a specific object, for example asking her to point to a cup. When Thalia was able to point to the cup, she received verbal praise from Lisa, "great job!" Lisa often exchanged a high-five with Thalia as well.

Correct responses earned Thalia a reward token in the form of a sticker. The reward tokens are designed to reinforce the desired behavior so that it can be learned and repeated. Thalia had to feel motivated to learn if the sessions with Lisa were going to be successful. Lisa had to figure out which behavior reinforcers worked for Thalia. The slightest adjustment to the learning program or the motivating reinforcer reward could increase a child's correct responses in therapy and, therefore, produce better behavior outcomes. Early on, the stickers paired with verbal praise were effective in getting Thalia to positively respond.

Lisa then rearranged the objects so that Thalia was recalling the object itself, rather than where the object was placed. Lisa would once again ask Thalia to point to the cup. Lisa did not waste time in between asking the behavior-prompting questions to maintain Thalia's attention. It also might take time for a child to respond to a simple identification request. The delay could be due to a child's uncertainty about the correct answer or a child's inability to stay focused. Thalia earned another reward token along with verbal praise if she again correctly pointed to the cup.

Lisa followed the learning program progression that she used at the DLC when working with Thalia. Lisa would add more objects so that there might be five or six to choose from before asking Thalia to identify the cup. Or, Lisa would have a different object be the theme of the learning program. Lisa might ask Thalia to identify a shoe with a picture of a cup still being one of the other object options placed in front of her. This technique helped Thalia learn a second object, a shoe, and ensured that she was not simply repeating the response of the first object that she was asked to identify, a cup. Different pictures of shoes or cups might be used to help Thalia learn that these items come in different shapes, colors, and sizes.

Thalia was given a one-or two-minute break when she achieved five reward tokens. Thalia would receive only one reward token for every five correct responses as she progressed. The break time cannot become greater than the learning time if a child starts to rapidly and correctly respond to prompting requests. Lisa set up a visual token board where Thalia could see how many more tokens she needed to earn before she was awarded a break. Seeing the token board became another source of motivation for Thalia.

Tricia became Thalia's playmate during her breaks. Thalia immediately ran out of the workroom to Tricia when she reached the needed number of reward tokens, often greeting her with a big hug. Tricia would pick up Thalia and give her a piggyback ride, or they played with an item from Thalia's basket of toys. Thalia loved to go outside and Tricia would take her to the backyard for her brief respite from her schooling. A timer was set to indicate when the break was over and Thalia had to return to a learning session.

Thalia occasionally threw a brief tantrum at the beginning of the learning process when having to do her therapy sessions, especially after a break. Thalia would drop to the floor or she sometimes swiped the learning materials off of the table. Thalia was also very aware of Tricia being there and she wanted to play with her. Working to better verbalize, Thalia referred to Tricia as, "Dish." Lisa became, "Seeda." Thalia would scream, "I want Dish" when she did not want to continue doing a learning session. Thalia was ready to play. Lisa would explain to Thalia when she had a tantrum or she delayed getting back to work that the playtime breaks were awarded only when she completed her therapy sessions to once again get her motivated.

The intensive work with short-earned breaks was the schedule every weekday from approximately nine o'clock in the morning until between one and two o'clock in the afternoon. The learning programs routinely continued while they were eating lunch. Orlando would return to Donnie and Lorena's house to pick up Thalia and watch his granddaughter until her parents got home from work.

Lisa came up with the idea of videotaping the therapy sessions instead of merely explaining to Donnie and Lorena what she was doing with Thalia. Tricia filmed the sessions between Lisa and Thalia. Lisa provided a narration for the video when she began a new learning program. Lisa explained how to conduct a therapy session and what that specific learning program was intended to achieve.

Lorena would watch the videos and repeat the lessons with Thalia later that evening. This work gave Thalia an additional one to two hours of daily therapy. The nightly learning sessions were a reflection of Lorena's desire to be part of the solution for her daughter. The additional therapy sessions were not only helpful for Thalia, but they were incredibly meaningful for Lorena.

Lisa would talk to Lorena or leave a note indicating if there was a specific skill that she could work on with Thalia at night. Lisa also showed Lorena how to use the reinforcer rewards when Thalia properly responded to requests. Lorena was then communicating to Lisa the nightly behavior of Thalia. This information helped Lisa know if Thalia was responding during only the daytime learning sessions or if she was transferring these lessons throughout her daily actions.

Building on the learning successes from the previous day was essential. Data were recorded for each learning program, at times another task of Tricia. The next, more advanced learning program was introduced when Thalia demonstrated that she mastered a certain skill. For example, once Thalia showed that she could consistently identify one object, a cup, she would be asked to point to multiple objects in the next learning program, a cup and a shoe.

Similarly styled learning programs were introduced to help Thalia identify and recognize letters, numbers, and colors. Lisa again started slowly by putting out only three pictures of solid colors. Lisa stated the name of each color. Lisa asked Thalia to identify a specific color and hand her that picture. Lisa pointed to the correct color and asked Thalia again if she hesitated or gave a wrong answer.

Lisa taught Thalia to identify and recognize and name the many gross motor skills by first using verb cards that had a picture of a child doing a specific action, such as standing, clapping hands, jumping, or waving. Lisa placed one verb card in front of Thalia, for example a girl waving, and she asked her, "what is she doing?" Thalia had to respond by saying the correct action. Lisa would prompt Thalia to do the action by asking her, "can you show me?" Thalia had to wave to complete the response. Lisa continued helping Thalia learn these actions by putting three different verb cards in front of her and asking her to point out and then perform a specific action.

The learning progression was for Lisa to try to get Thalia to identify actions through only verbal directions and not have the picture prompt. Thalia could not distinguish between clapping hands and standing up just from Lisa saying those actions when they started working together. Lisa demonstrated and named the action. She and Thalia then clapped hands and stood up together several times before Thalia started to differentiate and learn them.

Lisa used the same approach to teach Thalia to perform basic daily action requests that Donnie and Lorena might ask her to do. Lisa demonstrated to Thalia how to shut the door and turn off the light. The learning program became Thalia completing these actions through a verbal request. Lisa would ask Thalia to complete several actions consecutively as she advanced in this learning program before she earned her reward token.

Lisa moved from identification and recognition to the behavior objective of teaching Thalia to properly request an object. This request process began by getting Thalia to properly point to an object instead of grabbing and lunging for it. Lisa held objects that Thalia desired. Lisa would look away and remove the object from Thalia's sight if she grabbed aggressively for the object once she saw it. Again, Lisa was trying to instill age-appropriate behaviors. Thalia would get to play with that object for one or two minutes as the reinforcement reward if she properly pointed to the object.

Lisa would say the name of the object once a proper pointing request was made, for example "book." Lisa's saying the name of the object was designed to help Thalia later verbalize a request for that object. Lisa engaged Thalia in communication about the object during this time. Lisa would refer to some of the pictures if the object was a book. This conversation would reinforce a verbal and visual communication connection of words with pictures.

A snack could be used as a reward in these request learning programs as well. Thalia performing an action or making a proper object request could result in her earning a single M&M candy. It was Thalia, as with other children, who is ultimately deciding the motivating reinforcer. The reward token system or object play is a successful motivator of learning only if the teacher is offering a reinforcer that emits the behavior of the child that is trying to be produced.

Lisa later created a table of motivating reward items that Thalia could see as she did her learning programs. The table had items that Thalia liked to play with or eat. Thalia's table included fruit as the food item, a cup of juice, a doll, a Winnie the Pooh stuffed toy, and an animal book. She earned these items when she completed her work.

The reward system was implemented to help Lorena get Thalia to complete other everyday tasks. Thalia hated to have her toenails cut. Just seeing the toenail clipper or Lorena opening the drawer where it was kept could cause a tantrum-like reaction. Thalia was starting to have a reaction when Lorena went near that drawer. Ice cream was used as the motivating reward for Thalia in this instance. The starting point was that Thalia would earn a spoonful of ice cream if she stayed in her seat when just showing her the nail clipper. The next step was to have the nail clipper touch her toes for the ice cream reward to be obtained. The final step was to cut her toenails before the ice cream was earned.

Lisa videotaped a demonstration of her cutting Thalia's toenails. Lisa attempted to make it a fun activity. Lisa praised Thalia as she took off each of her sneakers by herself. When Thalia had trouble getting one sock off, she said to Lisa, "help me." Lisa then gave Thalia a Teletubbies toy to hold and play with. Lisa was communicating with Thalia about the toy to distract her. Lisa was singing the Teletubbies theme song and naming all of the characters. While Lisa was engaging Thalia, she gently touched each of Thalia's toes with the nail clipper. Lisa was able to cut Thalia's toenails without incident with her feeling comfortable and entertained. Lisa was praising Thalia the entire time by saying to her, "good girl, good sitting." Lisa turned it into a celebration when she was finished by asking Thalia for a high-five and telling her to show Tricia. Thalia gladly complied. Tricia offered verbal praise to Thalia by telling her how pretty she looked.

Ice cream was also used as the motivating reward to get Thalia to tolerate wearing a band-aid. Thalia's having to wear a band-aid caused her to scream and cry. Lisa started by just showing Thalia a band-aid. Thalia was awarded a spoonful of ice cream if she remained calm. Lisa then had the band-aid touch Thalia's skin for her to get some ice cream. The band-aid was then placed on Thalia's body for her to earn the ice cream. Lisa again turned it into a celebration when Thalia successfully was wearing the band-aid with verbal praise and a high-five.

Thalia adapted well to the work environment and the system of learning that Lisa created. Lisa felt that she established a rhythm with Thalia for these therapy sessions and that there was good pacing and progression of her learning. Lisa found Thalia to be an excellent learner. Thalia was understanding the concepts that she was being taught in this focused, one-on-one setting.

Lisa was equally pleased with the way that Thalia responded to the reward token system. It did not take long for Thalia to feel motivated in the working therapy sessions knowing that there was a reward when she completed her tasks. Thalia was becoming more attentive every day. Lisa's confidence was growing about how to best improve Thalia's skills. Any pressure that Lisa felt when starting to work with Thalia was immediately relieved because Thalia responded well. Lisa loved working with Thalia. After all of the months that Lisa had feelings of despair about Thalia's behavior, it was a rewarding experience for Lisa to help her young cousin.

CHAPTER 10

LISA SOON MOVED BEYOND WORKING ON THALIA'S RECEPTIVE communication skills and her properly pointing requests to focus on improving her expressive communication. Both receptive and expressive communication skills are part of understanding and processing language. Lisa began teaching Thalia receptive and expressive language in her communication of everyday items. Lisa placed several items on a table, such as different utensils, a cup, and a sock. Lisa then made a, "give me," request to Thalia. For example, Lisa stated, "give me the fork," in a test of Thalia's receptive communication. Lisa would offer verbal praise when Thalia gave her the fork. Lisa might say to Thalia, "good girl," or, "you are so smart." Lisa would then ask Thalia, "what did you give me?" Thalia had to respond to Lisa, "a fork," as a form of expressive communication. This learning program continued working on Thalia's receptive communication and the identification and recognition of objects, but now with an equal emphasis on her expressive communication.

Lisa did more extensive learning programs that combined receptive and expressive communication by introducing differentiation concepts to Thalia, for example in, under, and on. Lisa first taught Thalia what was meant by the word, in. Lisa set up two clear plastic cups for this learning program. One cup was turned upside down. Lisa gave Thalia a tiny toy bear. She instructed Thalia to, "put the bear in the cup," to work on her receptive communication. Lisa gave Thalia verbal praise when she properly put the bear in the cup. Lisa then asked Thalia, "where is the bear?" Thalia had to respond by saying, "in the cup," to develop her expressive communication. This back-and-forth testing about the word, in, was repeated several times before the concepts of under and on were introduced.

Lisa implemented a learning program to help Thalia distinguish between big and little by using two different-sized stuffed toy bunnies. Lisa first taught Thalia which was the little bunny and which was the big bunny by holding each one up for her to see and saying, "this is the big bunny," and, "this is the little bunny." With both bunnies on the table, Lisa would instruct Thalia to, "touch the little bunny." A correct response was rewarded with Thalia playing with that toy bunny.

Lisa's plan was to build to Thalia independently requesting items, not merely responding to prompts. Lisa wanted to teach Thalia to start to initiate communication and express her wants and needs. Lisa was trying to get Thalia to learn how to label her environment. This communication skill could be demonstrated through the use of, "I want," or, "I see," sentences. This was the next learning stage of Thalia moving away from the improper act of grabbing for the desired item when she saw it, to properly pointing to the item, to the use of words to request an item.

Lisa used an animal book that Thalia loved in this communication learning program. Each page of the book had a picture of a different animal. The book had a plastic extension on its side with a picture of each animal's face that made the sound of that animal when it was pushed. Lisa would point to an animal, for example a bird, and ask Thalia, "what do you see?" Thalia would have to say, "I see a bird." Lisa offered encouraging praise if Thalia correctly responded by saying to her, "I like the way you are talking," or, "nice job using your words." If Thalia responded by saying only the word "bird," but not in a sentence using the words, "I see," Lisa might just stare at Thalia until she said it correctly. The ultimate objective was to get Thalia to start communicating what she saw in a natural setting without any prompt. When Thalia observed a bird in real life and said, "I see a bird," it would be expressive communication that is logical and relevant to what she was experiencing.

Lisa would similarly stare at Thalia during a learning session if she grabbed for an item or she said the name of the item without saying, "I want." It would take for Thalia to use the words, "I want," before Lisa granted the request. Lisa would offer praise to Thalia when she made a proper request, such as "thank you for telling me what you want."

Lisa gave Thalia a toy or a food item that she requested almost every time she asked for it using the words, "I want." There is often no better reinforcer for a child to a properly stated, "I want," request than receiving that item. The amount that a child talks is increased when he or she learns that the item will be received by properly asking for it. Instilling a motivation for communicating using appropriate language is the objective.

Lisa started to incorporate an, "I want," request into Thalia's receiving her reinforcer reward. Lisa had been trying to help Thalia learn her name. Lisa would often say as a form of verbal praise to a learning program, "Yea, Thalia!" Lisa's constantly saying, "Thalia," was a strategy for her to better recognize her name. The next step was for Thalia to begin saying her name. Thalia was calling herself, "Tatee." Lisa decided to first try to get Thalia to say, "Tia," and then eventually say her full name. Lisa showed Thalia pictures of herself and asked her, "who is this?" Every time that Thalia responded, "Tia," Lisa offered her praise and a reward.

Lisa used the Winnie the Pooh stuffed toy as the motivator for this combined learning program to help Thalia say her name and properly make an, "I want" request. Thalia came to expect to play with her desired toy after correctly saying, "Tia," in her name learning program. Lisa was now having Thalia ask for the reward. Lisa gave Thalia the Winnie the Pooh stuffed toy only if she asked to play with it using, "I want." On one occasion when Lisa did not automatically give Thalia the toy for saying her name, Thalia said, "Pooh," but she did not use, "I want." Lisa stared at Thalia. Thalia said, "Pooh" again in a louder voice and elongating the word, "Poooooooh!" Lisa did not budge. A couple of seconds later, Thalia was able to figure out that she had to say, "I want Pooh." Lisa then gave Thalia the stuffed toy.

Lisa used the combination of an, "I want," request and the motivation of receiving that object to help Thalia learn to establish eye contact with another person. Thalia might make an, "I want," request as part of a learning program. Lisa would say her name, "Thalia," to get her attention and then stare at her. It was when Thalia looked at Lisa and held the eye contact that she received her requested object.

Lisa also worked on delayed gratification as part of an, "I want," learning program. There are times when a child's, "I want," request cannot be immediately granted because a parent is attending to another matter at that very moment. A parent might have to tell a child to, "wait a second," before fulfilling the request. Lisa was trying to teach Thalia that an, "I want" request might have to be slightly delayed and for her to not have a tantrum as a reaction. Lisa would ask Thalia to perform an action, such as clapping hands or standing up, before giving her the requested item after using "I want" to practice this concept. This small adjustment to the learning program teaches the child that a delay is possible in the, "I want," request process.

Similarly, parents might not always be immediately available to be next to their child to play. Lisa made a video for Lorena explaining how to create and use a picture activity book that guided Thalia on a series of items that she could play with. The activity book helped Thalia learn to play independently in the moments when Lorena could not play with her daughter. Lorena could instruct Thalia to do the activity book as she was getting ready for work or if she was cooking dinner.

The book featured a picture of an activity or an item that Thalia enjoyed playing with on each page. Thalia's activity book had a picture of blocks, a puzzle, a book that she liked to look at, and one of her favorite stuffed animals. The actual items pictured in the activity book were lined up against a wall. Thalia would independently retrieve the first pictured item and play with it. As Thalia turned the page in the activity book and she saw the next picture, she would play with that item. The last page of the activity book might be a picture of Thalia eating a certain snack. That snack would be in a bowl at the end of the items lined up against the wall to keep Thalia motivated.

Thalia's progress during the summer was immediate, consistent, and noticeable. Donnie and Lorena felt that they were starting to have their daughter revert to how she used to act. They had great joy and emerging feelings of relief. Their worst fears might not materialize. Thalia began to talk more. She started to verbalize her wants and needs without any prompting. Lorena also got to hear the phrase that she desperately wanted. Lorena cried when Thalia once again said, "I love you, mommy."

Orlando began arriving at Donnie and Lorena's house earlier in the afternoon. Thalia would not know that Orlando was there. It reached a point in her progress that he enjoyed listening in on Lisa working with his granddaughter. Orlando, who was with Thalia every day, noticed the improvement. He was seeing Thalia act like a kid again. Orlando became very excited when he heard Thalia say her name. He was even more excited upon hearing Thalia refer to him as, Abuelo.

One last lesson that Lisa did with Thalia at the request of Lorena was for her to learn how to blow out a candle in anticipation of her third birthday in August. Lisa taught Thalia how to sing "Happy Birthday" and for her to blow out the candle at the appropriate time at the conclusion of the song. Lisa sat Thalia in a chair. Lisa then lit the candle and they started to sing. Lisa gently put her hand on Thalia's stomach to indicate that she had to wait as Thalia tried to rise from her chair to blow out the candle before the song was finished. Lisa removed her hand as the song ended and Thalia successfully blew out the candle. Lisa cheered Thalia loudly when this occurred. Thalia wanted to continue singing "Happy Birthday" and blowing out the candle. It was one of her new favorite games.

Telling Lorena, "I love you," calling Orlando, "Abuelo," and singing "Happy Birthday," were all communication acts that did not occur a few weeks earlier. Lisa's therapy sessions with Thalia over the summer were a resounding success.

CHAPTER 11

DONNIE AND LORENA PURCHASED A HOUSE IN UNION, NEW Jersey in January 1995. It was a few months before their wedding in April. They were excited to share their first house. Planning to start a family was very much on their minds when they decided to buy this particular house. The house was located close to where Lorena worked. It was approximately twenty minutes from where each of their parents lived. The house had a nice-sized backyard and it was within walking distance of a diner, an ice cream shop, and a park. Donnie and Lorena could envision the days of taking their child to play at the park and then walking for ice cream.

A decision needed to be made as to where Thalia would receive her schooling in September. This was a prominent focus for Donnie and Lorena during the summer that Lisa was working with Thalia. Donnie and Lorena were going to be interacting with the Union school district in determining Thalia's education plan with

Thalia turning three years old in August, not the New Jersey state agency. The New Jersey Early Intervention Service coordinator wrote to Donnie and Lorena as she closed out Thalia's file, stating, "your ability and desire to advocate for Thalia's best interest is truly exceptional, and the incredible support you provide Thalia with so clearly results in her achievements."

The third pediatric neurologist emphasized in the report of Thalia's visit that an evaluation by the school district's child study team should be conducted as soon as possible to secure the proper education placement for September. A child study team generally consists of a child's teachers, a speech and language specialist, a school social worker, a school psychologist, and school or district administrators. These school officials work with the child's parents to develop and agree to an Individualized Educational Program, IEP. The Individuals with Disabilities Education Act requires that an IEP be created for each special education student.

An IEP is a document that presents the specific support services that will be provided by the school district to the child, as well as the rationale for these strategies. It describes the child's current academic skills and explains how the disability impacts his or her ability to learn. An IEP describes how much time and in what type of classroom environment certain education support services will be delivered. It also outlines the expected achievement outcomes for the child during the school year.

There is a case manager who oversees the child study team. The case manager is responsible for consulting with the child's general education and special education teachers to ensure the implementation of the IEP. The case manager monitors the child's progress and coordinates periodic meetings between the child study team and the child's family to review and revise the IEP as needed. An annual IEP meeting near the end of the school year is customarily part of this process. This meeting discusses the child's progress and plans the support services for the following school year. Parents can reach out to the case manager if they are having an issue with their child's education plan or progress. Parents can request a meeting with the child study team if desired.

A local school district in New Jersey has three options for a child who requires special education services. It can place a child in a general education, mainstreamed classroom in the district with support services being provided, such as a teacher's aide or individualized speech therapy. It can place a child in a special education classroom in the district, with additional support services being provided remaining a possibility. The final option is to secure an out-of-district school placement that specializes in that child's needs. Most school districts did not have classrooms set up for pre-kindergarten-aged children when Thalia was turning three years old. Certainly, most school districts did not have a classroom that was designed for children who had an autism spectrum diagnosis.

Donnie and Lorena had to find a school for Thalia to start in September as Union did not have an in-district pre-kindergarten classroom option for a child with her needs. Lisa obviously recommended the DLC to Donnie and Lorena. Thalia made substantial progress through her summer treatment. Lisa was highly confident in the DLC's ability to effectively continue this growth. The teachers at the DLC would be implementing the same applied behavior analysis techniques of individualized instruction, positive reinforcement through motivating rewards, and a progression of learning that was based on Thalia's performance data. Lisa thought that Thalia would respond well to the familiarity and structure of this teaching method. The adjustment would be Thalia having to physically go to the DLC school building rather than receiving the therapy sessions in her house.

The timing was fortuitous. Classes were opening at the DLC for children who were higher functioning on the autism spectrum, as they were starting to be routinely diagnosed. The higher-functioning children generally displayed some language skills. This class perfectly matched Thalia's skill set and her needs. A spot in that higher-functioning classroom was also available.

Lisa wanted Lorena to visit the DLC to see its classroom environment and understand its system of education. The DLC would be the school that Thalia attended for the next two years if everything went well. Lisa knew that for Lorena, as well as any other parent, this was not the plan that she visualized for her daughter. The acceptance of the situation is a constant and to some degree never completely goes away, invoking itself at different times with different intensity. Lisa understood that the visit to the DLC was the latest in what had been a series of emotionally difficult days for Lorena.

Lisa knew that Lorena had not seen anything like what she was about to witness at the DLC. Lisa bluntly told Lorena, "you are not going to like what you see." Lisa cautioned Lorena that what she was about to experience was not a typical preschool. Lisa asked Lorena to keep an open mind. She repeatedly told Lorena that this was exactly the type of school that Thalia needed. Lisa warned Lorena of the behaviors that she was about to observe. Lisa told Lorena that any comparison to another child should not matter and to not be worried about the array of problematic behaviors that some of the other children displayed. Lisa continued to point out to Lorena that Thalia's education was going to be individualized with one-on-one instruction.

It was easy for Lorena to notice during the visit that some of the children were in a more severe position on the autism spectrum than Thalia. Lisa had a concern that seeing these children could produce a response from Lorena that the DLC was not the right school for Thalia. Lisa experienced where parents would immediately reject what they saw at the DLC and think that their child's disability was not as extreme by comparison. These parents would claim that their child did not belong with the other, more seriously disabled children.

Lisa felt that the parents were getting in the way of their child's progress in most of these instances because they were refusing to acknowledge the reality of their child's situation. Lisa wanted to make sure that Donnie and Lorena continued to be accepting of what was needed to help Thalia. She did not want Donnie and Lorena to drift into any state of denial that would hinder Thalia's development.

Lorena cried when she first saw the DLC classroom. As Lisa could have predicted, Lorena had thoughts that Thalia's disability was not as dire as the other children's. Lorena questioned how Thalia might react in this environment. Was Thalia going to cry if she had to go to this school and be with people that she was not familiar? Would Thalia feel abandoned? Lorena briefly pondered at that moment if she should stop working to be with her daughter full-time.

Lisa again emphasized to Lorena how far Thalia progressed in her education and behavior therapy throughout the summer. Lisa added that the focused learning approach by the well-trained staff at the DLC would lead to continued success. Lorena knew that there were noticeable, positive changes in Thalia's behavior. Lorena became more agreeable to the idea of Thalia attending the DLC by the end of the day with all of Lisa's reminders, although she certainly remained apprehensive.

Lorena would simply be unsettled if she and Donnie were making the right decision for Thalia until they saw that she was comfortable in school. There was no possible way for absolute confidence that Thalia would thrive in this environment prior to her starting. The other reality was that Thalia had to receive her schooling in September somewhere. If not at the DLC, another school would be needed. Donnie and Lorena agreed to enroll Thalia at the DLC. They had to get the Union school district to consent to that request.

CHAPTER 12

THE REPRESENTATIVES OF THE UNION CHILD STUDY TEAM conducted an extensive information-gathering process to assess Thalia's skill level in determining her schooling plan. Evaluations by a school district social worker, a speech and language specialist, and a special education teacher were completed. The report of Thalia's third visit to the pediatric neurologist in May was also included in the child study team's assessment.

The evaluation by the speech and language pathologist occurred on July 18. It was only a few weeks into Lisa and Thalia's therapy sessions. Thalia was reluctant to go with the examiner to start the assessment. The examiner had to play several games of hide-and-go-seek with Thalia to get her to be somewhat comfortable. The examiner then offered Thalia a Blue's Clues toy, a popular children's television program on Nickelodeon that had an adult, Steve, who interacted with a cartoon dog, Blue. Thalia spontaneously shouted, "notebook," in reference to the notebook that appeared on the Blue's Clues toy that she was given, and the item that was frequently mentioned in the cartoon. Thalia became calmer playing with the toy. She soon walked with the examiner to the testing room.

The examiner first tried to get Thalia to sit down and identify objects by pointing to pictures. Thalia was not cooperative. The examiner then tried to get Thalia to follow simple instructions. Thalia was inconsistent. Thalia was able to stand up, touch her head, and touch a hat. She would not clap her hands, sit down, or give the examiner specific objects when she was asked to do so. Thalia showed that she could perform many of these acts during her sessions with Lisa. Thalia did not reply to all of the doable requests of the examiner on this day.

Non-responses present a challenge for any evaluation of this nature. The examiner has to figure out if a child is truly not capable of doing what is being asked, or if a child is unwilling to complete the task. A child may not be comfortable enough to perform the act in this environment. A child may prefer only to talk about the subject or play with the object that is of singular fascination. Some children exhibit being selectively mute, talking to their parents with whom they are familiar, but not the examiner. The tool of the examiner in this predicament is to be comprehensive in offering many different approaches to try to stimulate the child's behavior during the assessment.

Thalia rarely spoke when she was questioned, nor when she was asked to repeat words during the examination. Thalia did offer some spontaneous language, but it was only one word or a common phrase. Thalia eventually started to speak as she became relaxed in this testing environment. Several adults and children passed by Thalia and the examiner in the hallway at one point during the evaluation. Thalia consistently greeted each one by saying, "hi," or, "bye-bye."

The examiner tried to take away the Blue's Clues toy that she gave Thalia at the beginning of the evaluation. Thalia pushed the examiner's hand away. Thalia said, "don't do that," as the examiner repeatedly sought to remove the toy from Thalia's hand. The examiner asked Thalia to identify the clock and the crayons that were on the Blue's Clues toy. Thalia did not respond. The examiner attempted to get Thalia to say the words, clock and crayon, after being told what they were. Thalia's verbalization of those words was unintelligible.

The examiner thoroughly assessed Thalia's play skills. Several scenarios of pretend play were created as part of the evaluation. Thalia was able to give a toy bear, the examiner, and herself a pretend cup of juice when she was asked to do so. Thalia was not able to state when the bear was sleeping. Thalia offered up an utterance of, "shh," when the examiner told her that the bear was sleeping. Thalia picked up the bear and said, "hi bear," a few minutes later.

Thalia did not respond to all of the examiner's attempts to get her to play with some of the other toys or dolls. The examiner prompted Thalia to play with toys representing fruit. Thalia spontaneously said, "apple." Thalia mumbled, "nana," and, "gayk," when the examiner asked her to identify bananas and grapes. The examiner was not successful in getting Thalia to help her put the fruit toys back in their basket. Thalia did not respond when she was requested to complete that task.

Thalia showed that she understood how a cause-and-effect toy worked as she knew to push down a button for a character to pop up. Playing with that toy was of little interest to Thalia and did not last long. Thalia was unable to stack toy rings despite her watching several demonstrations by the examiner of how to perform that act.

The examiner was finally successful in taking and hiding the Blue's Clues toy from Thalia. The examiner continued to prompt

Thalia to play with other toys. Thalia indicated that she wanted to play with blocks by telling the examiner, "open," as she recognized a bag that would contain those items. There were, however, no blocks in that particular bag. Thalia repeated the examiner who said, "where are the blocks?" Thalia then repeated, "go get it," when the examiner pointed to another bag of blocks that she could play with. This was Thalia displaying her problematic communication tendency of mimicking language. Thalia appropriately played with the blocks. She correctly responded when the examiner asked her to place the blocks on top of, next to, and under the table.

The examiner then asked Thalia to pick out a toy that she wanted to play with. Thalia pointed to a puzzle that was in front of her and she said the word, "puzzles." Thalia began playing with a clock puzzle. Thalia started to incorrectly place some of the pieces in the puzzle. Thalia moved the pieces slightly in the same direction as the examiner verbally instructed her to turn the pieces around. Thalia again repeated the examiner's speech by saying, "turn it around." Thalia made several attempts to place the pieces properly in the puzzle. Thalia spontaneously said, "no go," to indicate that the puzzle piece did not fit in the space in the way that she was trying to place it. Thalia eventually said, "help me," to the examiner. The examiner asked Thalia to identify the colors of the puzzle pieces. Thalia correctly recognized orange, but she referred to all of the other colors, blue, red, and yellow, as green.

The examiner got Thalia to enthusiastically participate in singing hand-gesture-oriented songs. Thalia sang and performed all of the corresponding hand gestures to, "Wheels on the Bus." She continued to fill in the sounds when the examiner purposely stopped singing. Thalia knew what sound a cow made and she said it at the appropriate time as they sang, "Old McDonald." Thalia got stuck and she repeated the sound that a cow makes at the parts of the song where the sound of a pig or another animal was to be made.

The examiner picked up a play phone, presented it to Thalia, and asked her to talk to mommy. Thalia did not respond by grabbing the phone, but rather upon hearing the word, mommy, said, "I want go." The examination ended.

Lorena had an interview with a social worker from the school district on July 24, 2000. Lorena indicated in the interview that Thalia was making progress during the intense daily therapy that she was receiving from Lisa and the nightly work that she was doing with her daughter. Lorena told the social worker that Thalia was more alert and more aware of the people and things in her environment. Lorena said that Thalia was more frequently looking at the person who was talking to her. She added that Thalia was responding when someone called her name. It was noted that there was an improvement in Thalia's communication and her ability to recognize some words and numbers.

Lorena reported to the social worker that Thalia could be shy in a large group of people and that it takes time for her to feel comfortable. Lorena explained that Thalia's transition to nursery school was difficult in the early months. She described that Thalia often did not want to be around the other children. Thaila would play by herself. Lorena informed the social worker that interacting with the other children during playtime at nursery school did finally start to improve.

Lorena then offered some insight into Thalia's behavior at home. She explained that Thalia responded well to structure. Lorena said to the social worker that Thalia listened and followed the rules of the house. Lorena did mention that Thalia could have a five to ten-second tantrum when she did not get her way.

An assessment meeting was held on August 10, between

Lorena, Lisa, and seven representatives of the school district who comprised Thalia's child study team. It was concluded that Thalia's learning capabilities were being adversely affected by her autistic symptomatic behaviors. The highlighted characteristics of concern were delays and inconsistency in Thalia's receptive and expressive communication. The features of Thalia's expressive language were that she repeated words and her spoken phrases of more than one word were commonly heard sayings, such as "don't do that," or, "where'd it go?"

The social and emotional component of the evaluation revealed that Thalia did have some interest in engaging in imaginary play. Thalia would have a pretend tea party where she served her guests or play dress up where she put jewelry on herself and others or pretended to fix their hair. While this pretend play was encouraging, the overwhelming conclusion was that Thalia had socialization deficits that led to her more frequently engaging in parallel play. Thalia preferred to play next to other children rather than interact and play with them.

The evaluation by the child study team found that Thalia could be impulsive. She had difficulty focusing. She would sometimes incorrectly respond to instructions. Thalia's specific areas in need of improvement were defined as: trying to remain task-oriented, having social interactions with others in an acceptable manner, developing language skills, and demonstrating self-control. The evaluation pointed out that Thalia's behavior would not be a distraction to other students in a classroom. It was noted that Thalia's positive attitude was one of her behavioral strengths.

The effectiveness of the therapy sessions with Lisa was confirmed in her evaluation, despite Thalia's inconsistent performance with the school district's speech and language pathologist. Thalia's

Present Level of Performance Report showed that she was able to follow fifteen one-step directions, identify twenty common objects, and identify thirty pictures of common objects. Thalia was identifying basic everyday activity verbs in pictures, such as eating, sitting, waving, walking, crying, and washing. Thalia could point to ten body parts on herself, a doll, or another person. Thalia was just starting to express herself with, "I want," sentences. If Thalia was having a problem maneuvering an object, she might say, "help me," or, "it's stuck." Thalia was getting better at identifying shapes. She could sort objects by shape.

The conclusion of the child study team's evaluation officially declared that Thalia qualified for district-provided special education and related support services. The special education eligibility report stated that Thalia, "requires a highly specialized program with a strong language component to facilitate her total academic as well as social/emotional growth." This outcome was not surprising. The specific school placement and educational support services needed to be determined.

Lisa made Donnie and Lorena aware of a new role that they would have to fulfill, being an advocate for Thalia. There could not be an assumption on their part that the school district was going to handle every aspect of Thalia's case perfectly. Donnie and Lorena could not willingly accept only the services that were offered by the school district. They would have to be proactive in assuring that Thalia received as many support services as possible.

Donnie and Lorena put forth several requests to the school district in the crafting of Thalia's initial IEP. They asked that Thalia attend the DLC. They asked that Thalia receive individual speech therapy four times per week. A request was made that Thalia receive full-day, full-year schooling. Structure and repetition would be critical aspects of Thalia's progress. Children with learning disabilities are more likely to relapse quickly, making schooling during the summer necessary.

The school district approved Thalia attending the DLC. It was agreed that Thalia would receive individual speech therapy three times per week for thirty minutes. This was the number of days and the amount of time that the child study team's language and speech pathologist recommended. Donnie and Lorena's request that Thalia attend school in the summer was granted. The school district was to assume the transportation costs of busing Thalia to the DLC.

CHAPTER 13

O N September 6, 2000, the bus arrived at Donnie and Lorena's house shortly after seven o'clock in the morning to pick up Thalia for her first day of school at the DLC. Traveling by bus to the DLC was another considerable obstacle to overcome. Thalia had to get on a bus and ride to school without being accompanied by a parent, only two weeks after her third birthday.

Donnie and Lorena did have the option to drive Thalia to school, but it was strongly preferred by the DLC staff that the children take the bus. Having the children arrive at the DLC on the bus helped introduce structure to their day. It offered an initial opportunity for the children to have some independence simply by them walking from the bus into the school building.

Lisa encouraged Donnie and Lorena to have Thalia take the bus to the DLC. Lisa experienced when parents would drive their child to school and the child did not want to get out of the car. A parent might decide that it was easier to acquiesce to the child and return home rather than have the child cry, scream, or throw a tantrum. Another situation that might occur was when the parents walked their child into the school building and the child would not want to leave their side. The DLC was trying to establish a learning environment and to condition certain behaviors. The parents being at the school could be a distraction. It was mentioned to the parents that they could follow the bus and watch their child walk into the school building if that made them more comfortable. Lisa was able to convince Donnie and Lorena that there were benefits to having Thalia travel to the DLC on the school bus.

The first day of Thalia taking the bus to school was among the hardest for Lorena. It was traumatic for Lorena that Thalia's having to attend a specialized school at such a young age was even occurring. Lorena could pop into the classroom at any point and check on her daughter when Thalia was in nursery school. That, obviously, was no longer possible at this school. Lorena still had some uncertainty that the DLC was the appropriate school for Thalia, despite the understanding that she and Donnie had of Thalia's needs and the assurances from Lisa. Lorena could not help but once again question if this intensive learning environment was the right choice for Thalia now that the day of her starting school arrived. Lorena kept asking herself if she was putting Thalia through too much.

Thalia climbed aboard the bus when it arrived and she got into her booster seat without incident. Lorena fought through tears as she too got on the bus to introduce herself to the bus driver and the transportation aide who assisted the children. Lorena made sure that Thalia was buckled into her seat belt. Lorena told Thalia, "I love you, princessita," (little princess in Spanish – princessita was one of the special names that Lorena called Thalia, along with muneca, doll in Spanish). Lorena gave her daughter a kiss and a tight hug before she stepped off of the bus. Thalia just kept staring at Lorena through the window. Lorena tried not to cry as she looked at Thalia, but she sobbed as the bus pulled away.

Lorena tried to make it a point to not cry in front of Thalia. Lorena did not want to upset or scare Thalia. Lorena thought that if she appeared strong, Thalia would stay strong as well. Lorena saved some of her crying meltdowns for when she was at work or when Thalia could not see her.

Lorena took the day off from work. She knew that there was no way that she could focus on performing her job. Lorena called the DLC a few minutes after the bus left her house to make sure that it arrived at the school safely. Lorena spent most of the morning looking at the clock, pacing, and fighting the urge to call the school again to ask how Thalia was doing. Lorena could not resist very long and she called the school to speak with Thalia's teacher. Hearing from the teacher that Thalia was doing well on her first day of school was the only way for Lorena to feel slightly better during her tear-filled day.

A typical school day at the DLC consisted of small group sessions and individualized instruction. The school day began at 8:45 with circle time, a period when all of the children worked together on an activity, such as identifying that day's weather or singing hand-gesture-oriented songs. Each child would then receive his or her individualized education and behavior learning programs.

Thalia had eight students in her class. This number meant that the ideal staffing needs for the class were a teacher and seven teacher's aides. The DLC rotated the teacher's aides who worked with Thalia. While familiarity and structure were important, so too was getting a child to become comfortable interacting with many people. Having a different teacher's aide deliver a learning program helped evaluate if a child was responding only to one individual aide or if a child was truly learning the skills that were being taught. Perhaps, one teacher's aide was prompting a child too much during a lesson to receive positive results. There is greater confidence that a child is mastering a skill if a teacher's aide is switched and a child continues to perform that task.

Lunch was at 11:30 every morning. There was time for the children to play with their classmates after lunch. The children might play outside during this time if the weather was nice. The children would have physical education for forty-five minutes. There was more individualized instruction in the afternoon, which was followed by another period of circle time. The students would have an art or a music class on certain days. The school day ended at 2:45. The bus then drove the children home. Thalia did not get back to her house until approximately four o'clock in the afternoon to complete her nine-hour day of being away from her parents or the family members who would have watched her.

The teachers at the DLC communicated with Lorena through daily journals. Lorena could not simply ask her daughter basic questions and expect a response, such as "how was school?" Or, "what did you learn today?" Lorena received written communication from the teacher's aide who worked with Thalia on that day's individualized learning programs as well as from the speech therapist on the days that Thalia had a session. The teachers would write and explain what lessons they worked on during that particular day, what Thalia ate for lunch, how Thalia behaved, and make any requests for items that Lorena needed to put in Thalia's book bag. The note from the teacher's aide to Lorena on the first day of school on September 6, 2000, read in part, "Thalia had a great day. She has made a lot of progress with Lisa and she is going to do great in this class. She was shy this morning but became very social in the afternoon. She played next to other children and shared their toys. She showed us a lot of language this afternoon as well. I will continue to work on the programs that Lisa started."

Lorena provided a written response in the daily journal that was read by the teacher the next morning. Lorena would inform the teacher how Thaila behaved at night and what activities she did at home. The daily journal had a spot where Lorena could circle the areas that she wanted Thalia's teacher to comment on in the following day's writing. Among the options that Lorena could request information about were: academics, socialization, task completion, self-care, and speech. Lorena could initiate a phone call with Thalia's teacher at any point. She would use the daily journal to indicate that desire as well.

Lorena wrote back to Thalia's teacher after the first day, "thank you again for returning my call yesterday. If you can, keep in touch with me so I can continue her learning at home. I guess by now you can see that Thalia <u>loves</u> praise and encouragement." Lorena circled academics, task completion, and speech in the daily journal as the areas that she wanted to know more about the following day.

The daily journal provided Lorena with a sense of ease and understanding that would not have existed without that extensive communication. The teacher wrote on the second day of school, "Thalia did great today. She seems more comfortable in school today. She's getting out of her seat and getting silly. She has quite a personality. At lunch, she wants all of my attention. I tried to get her to talk to a peer. She smiles at him and says, 'hi,' but she's confused about what I want her to do. She'll catch on."

The speech therapist also wrote to Lorena as this day was the first session with Thalia. The speech therapist commented that Thalia, "was very responsive and social. I used this session to look at her articulation errors which I found to be very inconsistent, as you probably already know. Right now, I'm just trying to get to know Thalia, as well as her getting used to me."

The teacher provided Lorena with a list of the concepts that Thalia was working on in her individualized learning programs. Academically, it was teaching Thalia two-step directions, naming missing items, letter identification, sorting and putting like-objects in a pile, and differentiation of concepts, such as on or inside, big or little, and my or your. It was certainly helpful that Lisa introduced Thalia to some of these examples of differentiation. The teacher reported to Lorena that Thalia does get easily distracted so they would be doing exercises that helped her focus.

The speech therapist was working with Thalia on the articulation of her name, letter sounds, and trying to get her to pace her speech so that she can better pronounce words. Pacing became an issue when Thalia counted as well. Thalia would lose count or skip numbers because she was reciting the numbers at a fast pace. The teachers implemented a before and after learning program to help Thalia focus on counting and sequencing numbers. Thalia might be asked, "what number comes before three?" Speech therapy sessions also included efforts to get Thalia to appropriately answer, "when," questions and conversational questions, such as "how are you?"

The early social behavior learning programs focused on taking turns, sitting nicely, and reciprocating conversation and actions. Thalia worked on coloring and cutting to improve her fine motor skills. Finally, the DLC staff was coordinating with Lorena to get Thalia potty trained.

Lorena continued to use the daily journal in the first few days to help the DLC teachers get to better know Thalia. Among the notes that Lorena wrote to them was, "I hope she is not too much trouble. I know she tends to, at times, cling on and just wants a hug or a kiss." Lorena was able to offer helpful hints about Thalia. She wrote that Thalia loves ketchup, but she is unable to pronounce the word so she says, "something like coppy." Lorena informed the teachers that, "Thalia <u>loves</u> dresses. She is a real 'girl' and loves being told how pretty she looks."

Lorena used the daily journal to seek clarification about the learning system at the DLC. Lorena asked, "what does gross motor learning mean that Thalia is actually doing?" She also wanted to know, "is circle time when she gets together with her peers?" The teacher was then able to respond and explain to Lorena that gross motor learning is a structured gym class where the children work on age-appropriate skills of running, jumping, balancing, and riding bikes. Or, respond that circle time is when the students work on calendar skills, learn songs, and group directions with their peers.

Lorena wrote to Thalia's teacher as she was still adjusting to the structure of the DLC, "am I the only mother who asks so many questions? I'm sorry, I just want to be sure we are on the same wavelength." The teacher, of course, respectfully responded, "I don't mind your questions so if I don't have time to write answers to all, I'll call you." Thalia's teacher also spoke to Lisa within the first ten days of the school year.

Lorena asked the DLC staff for the learning programs that she could do at home with Thalia. Lorena cherished her evening time spent working with Thalia. These sessions were a way for Thalia to improve as well as a way for Lorena to feel that she was part of her daughter's learning and behavior development. Lorena informed the teacher that when Thalia gets home, "she appears a little tired so I don't know if I should continue to drill her." The teacher assured Lorena that, "so far, all the parents have reported that their children are exhausted when they get home from school. Thalia may just need some more time to adjust to a full day of school. Eventually, she should be able to work at home also."

The teacher explained to Lorena within one week of her starting at the DLC that Thalia is, "so happy when she comes into school." The teacher also indicated that every day Thalia is becoming more interested in her peers. The teacher elaborated that Thalia is, "imitating them and laughing at them when they're funny. She plays near them, but not with them yet." The teacher added that Thalia loved going to music class, although she was slightly frightened when the teacher put a stamp on her hand at the end of the first session. Thalia's taking some time before getting completely comfortable with all of the new experiences at the DLC was expected. The daily routines of getting on the bus, group time, and individualized learning, however, were getting established.

The DLC used a reward token system to reinforce positive behaviors. The individualized instruction with the visual reward token board brought familiarity to how Thalia learned all summer with Lisa. Thalia performed well in the early learning programs. She showed that she was capable of looking at pictures of children engaging in actions and telling the teacher what activity they were doing, such as running, walking, and swimming. This was another learning program that Thalia already worked on with Lisa.

Thalia tended to get nervous when she was working on a new and difficult learning program. One learning program that was challenging for Thalia was identifying what is missing. The teacher would show Thalia two objects before removing one of them and asking her to name what is missing. Thalia became upset as she struggled with this task. Lorena indicated to the teachers that Thalia will give a good effort, but that she gets upset when she cannot complete a task. Thalia would then get frustrated and start to lose focus on what the teacher was trying to get her to do in the learning program. The teacher wrote to Lorena and asked for suggestions for a highly motivating behavior reinforcer reward that will help Thalia stay focused during the more difficult learning programs. Lorena indicated that Thalia liked M&M's candy.

Thalia had some breakthrough moments early in the school year. Thalia was starting to initiate more spontaneous expressive communication. Thalia went for a speech therapy lesson one morning and she immediately pointed at the therapist's shirt and said, "orange." Thalia then pointed at her own shirt and said, "yellow." This type of typical expressive language represented a huge indication of progress. Some children on the autism spectrum never reach this point in their communication. Thalia showed that she was getting better at expressing herself by advancing to a level of communicating that had her labeling her environment. Thalia was no longer just responding when prompted by a teacher to state what she observed. Thalia was proactively communicating what she saw, such as the color of the speech therapist's shirt.

The learning programs in applied behavior analysis teaching are initially designed for a child to respond to a prompt and then receive verbal praise and a reward paired together upon a correct response. The objective of this approach is to gradually phase out the reward and have the student reinforced by just verbal praise. The next critical step is for a child to perform the behavior out of desire. A child is communicating because of a desire to have a social interaction. The behavior of engaging in communication is now the stimulating activity, replacing the self-stimulating behaviors that the child was doing. Just having a social interaction is the reward. Thalia was starting to more frequently experience this communication and social interaction sensation.

The teachers felt that Thalia's developmental delays in language and socialization impacted her ability to interact with peers at an age-appropriate level when she started at the DLC. The teachers were noticing that Thalia was becoming more comfortable interacting with her peers. The teacher reported on September 15 that Thalia was talking to her peers by using their names, chasing them around the room until they engaged with her, asking for items, and telling them, "no," when appropriate. The teacher wrote to Lorena on that day that the staff was amazed to see this. Another day, Thalia played outside with a classmate on the swings and they took turns going up and down the slide. They ran and chased each other around the playground. Thalia initiated conversation during their game of tag by telling her classmate to, "come get me," and, "I got you."

Thalia called out to a classmate on another occasion during group social time, "come here, come play." They began interacting in the play-kitchen area of the classroom. Thalia asked her classmate, "do you want a drink?" Upon the response of, "ok," Thalia said, "here you go, drink it." Thalia further initiated conversation with her teachers by telling them first thing when she arrived at school if she was wearing new sneakers, had a new bow in her hair, or if Lorena put a new color of polish on her fingernails. These were other significant social communication breakthrough moments of early progress.

Donnie and Lorena were seeing a difference in Thalia's behavior at home. Thalia was constantly singing the "Goodbye" song that the children sang at the end of the school day. Thalia behaved very well when she went to see her first movie in a theater, Disney's animated film, *The Emperor's New Groove*. The prospects of putting Thalia in other learning settings seemed appropriate. Donnie and Lorena enrolled Thalia in a weekend swimming class.

Lorena was starting to once again see a social comfort in Thalia's interactions with her cousins. Lorena and Janet took

Thalia and Deanna to see Sesame Street Live. Thalia loved the show. She was naming the characters and she kept wanting to move closer to the stage. Thalia and Deanna were holding hands as they walked. Thalia was talking to Deanna throughout the night. She often asked questions of her cousin. Lorena was thrilled to see this amount of interaction between Thalia and Deanna. Lorena repeatedly heard Lisa emphasize that playing and communicating with peers are such important characteristics and an indication of proper behavior development. It was ten months earlier at Grandma Morsillo's birthday party that Thalia displayed no interest in playing with Deanna.

Janet noticed that Thalia was no longer doing any self-stimulating behaviors. Janet observed Thalia being social with Deanna. The two kids were playing dress-up and other games. It was getting back to how they acted together before Thalia's autism disability characteristics emerged.

On October 12, 2000, five months after diagnosing Thalia as being on the autism spectrum, the third pediatric neurologist who assessed her once again conducted an evaluation. The doctor immediately noticed that Thalia made considerable progress. The doctor found Thalia to be very friendly and expressive. Thalia maintained better eye contact with the doctor during this examination than on the previous visit. Thalia was able to tell the doctor that she was three years old and that she was a girl when she was asked those questions. The doctor confirmed that Thalia was capable of speaking using short sentences and communicating her wants and needs using, "I want," directives. Thalia still had some difficulty focusing as the doctor tried to conduct some mental tests. Thalia was given a one-word picture vocabulary test in which she scored at the fourteenth percentile when compared to other same-aged children.

The report from the pediatric neurologist provided evidence that the therapy that Lisa performed over the summer, the evening sessions with Lorena, and the initial few weeks spent at the DLC yielded positive results. Age-appropriate behaviors that were not happening a few months earlier were regularly occurring. Behaviors that were of concern appeared with less frequency, or not at all. Lorena reported to the doctor that Thalia was not having any giggling episodes as she fell asleep. Lorena informed the doctor that Thalia was more sociable and comfortable in approaching other children to play, including children that she did not yet know all that well. The doctor concluded in the report of this visit that, "Thalia appears to be doing very well. She has certainly made considerable interim improvement." There was increasing optimism.

CHAPTER 14

THALIA CONTINUED TO PERFORM WELL THROUGHOUT HER first year at the DLC. Donnie and Lorena were now completely confident that Thalia was in the right school environment and that she was getting the educational assistance that she needed. They could see her learning and behavior progress. Donnie and Lorena were also pleased with the structure of the DLC.

Lorena was satisfied and greatly appreciative of the level of communication that she received in the daily journal from the DLC teachers and the speech therapist. Lorena wrote to the teacher and speech therapist in late January, "thank you for being so detailed and supportive with Thalia." A few months later, Lorena wrote, "thank you for your patience and dedication with my daughter." It was a genuine sentiment that Lorena could have conveyed daily. One day, the journal included a surprise for Donnie and Lorena. As Thalia watched her teacher writing to her parents, she said that she wanted to write a note too. "Hi mom and dad, love Thalia," was in the margin of that day's journal writing.

Thalia was becoming noticeably more communicative. On January 4, 2001, the speech therapist wrote to Lorena that Thalia was, "talking up a storm today," and that, "a lot of it was very functional," indicating that her communication had meaning and was on topic. Thalia repeatedly called out the speech therapist's name to get her attention during that day's session. The speech therapist turned around to Thalia and with a funny face and a funny tone of voice said, "what?" Later in the session when the speech therapist called Thalia's name, Thalia turned her head around and using the same funny face and funny tone of voice that the therapist used said, "what?"

Thalia was communicating if she needed an item at school, saying, "I need juice," "I need tissues," "I need a hug," and telling her teachers when she needed to use the bathroom. Thalia was communicating with the other children as well, such as saying to a classmate, "it's your turn," when appropriate. The speech therapist wrote to Lorena that Thalia, "really picks up what others say and she tries to use it correctly."

Thalia always responded well to praise and encouragement from the teachers. This might come in the form of them clapping their hands after a correct response or her receiving a hug. The teachers found Thalia to be motivated by behavior reinforcer rewards as well, especially Blue's Clues fruit snacks. The teachers were often writing to Lorena in the daily journal to send more fruit snacks because Thalia loved them so much and they helped maintain her focus when doing learning programs.

Thalia was quick to pick up on her teacher saying that more Blue's Clues fruit snacks were needed when Lorena forgot to send them on one occasion. Thalia reminded her mother when she got home, repeatedly telling her, "mommy, you forgot Blue's Clues fruit snacks." Thalia was excited when the teacher spotted her favorite snack in her book bag the next day. Thalia was motivated to work extra hard in her learning sessions to earn that reward. Thalia would also try to cleverly sneak an extra fruit snack by asking a teacher for a hug and while embracing reach for her desired treat. Thalia tried this maneuver with the different teacher's aides that worked with her for the first time. Lorena confirmed that Thalia tried this tactic with her as well, telling the DLC staff, "I know that trick."

The teacher and the speech therapist were using the daily journal to provide Lorena with the areas that she could work on with Thalia at home. Lorena dutifully helped her daughter as she was told what Thalia needed to improve. Thalia was having some trouble differentiating between identifying something as hot or cold during her lessons at school. The speech therapist suggested to Lorena that she teach this to Thalia by showing her items in her daily environment that are hot and cold, such as items in the freezer or the stove. Distinguishing between hot and cold water was another suggestion. At times, Thalia was better at identifying hot items and on other occasions, she was better at identifying cold items. It would not be until the end of March that the speech therapist wrote to Lorena that Thalia mastered hot and cold.

Distinguishing between in and on was another differentiation that was difficult for Thalia to completely grasp. Lisa introduced these concepts to Thalia, but refreshing what these words meant still needed to be done. The speech therapist indicated that Thalia had a better understanding of on. It was communicated to Lorena to help with teaching these concepts to Thalia. Under was introduced when the concepts of in and on were soon mastered.

Proper usage of mine and yours was also taught. The teacher would point to something on herself or Thalia and ask, "whose is it?" Thalia was saying her name or the teacher's name at the beginning of those lessons. It took Thalia a few tries before she was able to understand the concept and properly use mine or yours. Similarly, reciprocal conversation was introduced. The teacher might say, "I am twenty-three years old." Thalia was supposed to say that she is three years old. Thalia was repeating what the teacher said, "I am twenty-three years old." This too took some time before Thalia eventually started to properly respond.

The teachers and Lorena worked with Thalia to get her to learn her home address. Thalia quickly picked up on the name of her street, but with four numbers in her address, she often omitted one number or she confused the order. Thalia finally learned to correctly recite her home address after it was repeatedly drilled.

Other learning activities focused on following basic instructions. Thalia was told which picture to color and which color crayon to use. The learning programs were gradually getting harder, again introduced based on the performance data indicating that Thalia mastered one skill and that she was ready to advance to the next skill. Thalia was taught to speak in sentences. Thalia would be handed two objects by her teacher before being questioned, "what do you have?" Thalia had to respond in a full sentence, for example "I have a cup and a pencil."

There was much progress to detail to the Union school district child study team leading up to the group's IEP meeting scheduled for the end of January 2001. It was the child study team's first meeting since August. The IEP meeting was attended by Lorena, Lisa, three members from the school district, and three staff members from the DLC, Denise as the school's supervisor, Thalia's classroom teacher, and the speech therapist.

The representatives of the DLC presented the data to show that Thalia was grasping the concepts that she was being taught in her learning programs. Thalia's progress report indicated that she was matching upper and lower-case letters with one hundred percent accuracy. Thalia performed well when prompted with the question, "what do you see?" And, "what do you have?" She could respond to those questions in simple sentences beginning with, "I see," or, "I have." Thalia mastered some differentiation concepts, including distinguishing between big and little, wet and dry, clean and dirty, and tall and short. She could use the phrases, "my turn," and, "your turn," appropriately. Thalia's sorting of categories was demonstrated by her being able to separate pictures of foods, animals, clothes, and vehicles. The teacher might mix three or four animal pictures with a number of other non-animal pictures. Thalia would be required to stack all of the animal pictures in a pile.

Thalia was answering a minimum of five questions about herself. She was able to state her name, age, birthday, the names of family members, the name of her teacher, and the town where she lived. Thalia originally called the town, "Unie," before she learned to correctly pronounce, Union. Thalia's fine motor skills improved. She knew the materials to retrieve with minimal guidance when she was asked to cut, paint, or glue. She was able to perform all of these fine motor skills. Thalia might color a little outside of the lines or it might not be exactly on the line of a picture when she cut paper, but those were minor errors. Thalia's ability to complete hand-coordination activities was evident. Thalia's gross motor skills of running and jumping, which were never an issue, remained age-appropriate.

Thalia was displaying better social skills. She was more frequently participating in make-believe play that included cooking with pretend foods, talking on the telephone, or playing with dolls and toy animals. Thalia politely raised her hand during group sessions. She was sharing without being prompted. Thalia was navigating the lunch line, choosing a drink and a dessert, and carrying her tray without assistance. The teachers commented to Lorena that Thalia was self-sufficient. Thalia initiated conversations with her classmates during lunch. She commonly asked her classmates what they were eating, while informing them of what she was having for lunch.

Lorena reported to the child study team that she felt that Thalia was more observant and better at recognizing things in her environment. Thalia was talking more about what happened in her day. Lorena was hearing phrases that she knew that Thalia learned at school, such as one time telling her mother, "be quiet, it's not your turn." Thalia was singing the songs that she was taught in her music class. She told Lorena, "I love to sing." Donnie and Lorena were routinely serenaded by Thalia singing, "Itsy Bitsy Spider," "You are My Sunshine," and "It's a Small World." Thalia would tell Lorena when she tried to join in, "no mommy, don't sing."

The overall conclusion in the January IEP report was that "Thalia continues to make steady progress in the area of speech and language." The plan of the child study team was to continue exactly as is. Thalia had the remainder of the current year and one more full year of schooling at the DLC. While the Union school district was still responsible for following up on Thalia's education and conducting IEP meetings, the DLC would maintain discretion on the implementation of the specific daily learning and behavior programs for Thalia. The teaching methods based on individual instruction and the use of positive reinforcement were to remain. It was also recommended to allow frequent breaks, use visual demonstrations if needed, vary activities often, and provide structure. Thalia was to receive an extended school year in the summer. A concern lingered about Thalia regressing as a slight difference in her skills was detected after periods of extended vacation. The next IEP meeting with the child study team was planned to occur in one year, January 2002.

CHAPTER 15

THALIA BEGAN TO DISPLAY CERTAIN PERSONALITY TRAITS during her time at the DLC. Thalia wanted to do everything for herself. She strongly disliked when someone intervened to help her, even at this young age. Thalia would challenge herself to figure it out when she did not immediately know how to complete a task. She enjoyed finishing a task independently and being proud of what she accomplished. Thalia might ask a teacher to put a star or a sticker on a completed worksheet. Thalia was now telling Lorena as she started doing certain tasks at home, "no mommy, I'll do it."

Thalia's desire to work independently got to the point where sometimes at school she became determined to complete a difficult task all by herself that she would refuse any friendly assistance. Thalia was drawing on the chalkboard when a teacher tried to help her complete the picture. Thalia got upset because she wanted to finish the picture by herself. The teacher had to explain to Thalia that it is alright to have someone help her complete a project and that doing an activity together can be fun.

The teachers were confronted with some occasions where Thalia did not listen or follow their directions. These moments were rare and generally occurred when Thalia was a little tired. The teacher wrote to Lorena after one school day that Thalia did not do much work. The teacher described that Thalia seemed tired as she kept yawning. All Thalia wanted to do on that day was sit on one of the teacher's laps. Lorena confirmed in the daily journal that Thalia woke up that morning feeling a little, "crabby." Lorena was sure to do some learning programs with Thalia at home that evening upon hearing that she did not have a productive day at school. The teacher reported that the next day at school Thalia was, "a perfect angel all day."

Thalia could be resistant and tell a teacher, "no," and cry if she did not want to do what she was being asked. A teacher wanted Thalia to clean up the blocks that she was playing with after a playtime session. Three-and-a-half-year-old Thalia said to the teacher, "no, you clean it up." Thalia got upset and cried when the teacher again asked her to clean up the blocks. Thalia did eventually clean up the blocks herself once she saw that she was disappointing her teacher.

Progress continued, but at times it was a little slower than others. Auditory distinction was a learning theme of the speech therapist during the winter months. Thalia was having trouble distinguishing between words that sounded alike, such as towel and owl, or fish and dish. The speech therapist sent home worksheets with pairs of similar-sounding words for Lorena to practice with Thalia.

The speech therapist was continuing to try to get Thalia to slow down when speaking to help her better understand and pronounce words. The speech therapist during their sessions would slow down her own speech substantially and then prompt Thalia to imitate speaking at that rate. The speech therapist was consistently pleased with Thalia's effort. It was written to Lorena that Thalia, "is starting to develop self-monitoring skills. If you tell her that it wasn't said right, she will keep trying until it is right."

Another major area that the DLC teachers tried to get Thalia to improve was her recall of information. One strategy was for Lorena to write in the daily journal what Thalia had for dinner and dessert, which many times was a bowl of Jell-O with her father, and any activity that she did in the evening. Lorena was instructed to write if Thalia watched a movie or a television show, with Clifford the Big Red Dog and Scooby Doo among her favorites, and on occasion, she watched basketball with Donnie as he tried to teach her to say, "go Knicks." It was to be written in the daily journal when Thalia spent time coloring with Lorena or helping her bake cookies or banana bread, playing on the laptop computer that Donnie bought, or going outside to play and with whom. The activities were important for Lorena to describe because they provided more details that the teachers could ask Thalia about in testing her recall. The teachers gave Thalia hints to get her to give the correct answer if needed.

Similarly, with the teachers writing in the daily journal what Thalia ate for lunch and the activities that she participated in during the school day, Lorena was able to ask Thalia for her to recall that information. Lorena often asked Thalia general questions, such as what day of the week is it? Or, what is the weather like today? Lorena now tried every day to get Thalia to tell her something that happened at school. Lorena would ask Thalia the names of her friends at school that she played with or the name of the teacher's aide who worked with her that day.

Lorena started to test Thalia's recall of other events that occurred. Lorena had to take Thalia with her to work for two days when school was closed because of snow. Thalia had a fun time spending the days at work with her mother. Lorena first explained to Thalia that the people that she took care of were hurt and that they needed to feel better. Thalia showed her outgoing, friendly personality by telling the patients, "don't be sad," "you'll be ok," or, "I'll get a band-aid for the booboo." Many patients also received one of Thalia's loving hugs. Lorena asked Thalia questions at the end of the day when they got home. Thalia was able to successfully recall her day's activities. Thalia immediately told her teachers when she returned to school that she went to work with her mother.

The teachers were using several strategies throughout the school day to develop Thalia's recall. Thalia would be asked to perform a task and then quizzed five minutes later to tell the teacher what she did. Thalia was routinely directed by her teacher to go to another part of the classroom to retrieve two objects, testing her listening and recall. Thalia's teacher would read her a book and tell her about some of the pictures before Thalia had to recall what they discussed. The teacher might wait until the following day to ask Thalia to name one of the characters in the story that was read to her.

It was requested that Lorena indicate what Thalia ate for breakfast in the daily journal to test her more immediate recall. Thalia had some difficulty when the speech therapist first asked her what she had to eat for breakfast. The therapist was able to figure out that Thalia did not understand what the word, breakfast, meant as the name of the meal that she ate before coming to school in the morning. Thalia's ability to recall was to some degree a function of her level of focus. It was similar to how Thalia performed very well on her learning programs when she was focused. Thalia could have a problem with recall when she was not focused, even if she was given response choices.

Some of Thalia's learning programs were conducted in a two-child, one-teacher setting starting in March. This was another important moment of progress. This was a step to better prepare Thalia for learning in settings with more students. Thalia thrived in the two-child, one-teacher format. She was motivated when doing a learning program with one of her classmates. Thalia truly enjoyed being around her classmates. The teacher wrote to Lorena one day in the daily journal that Thalia, "played really nice with her peers today. She always wants to get someone to play with her. She loves the interaction." Thalia was comfortable with the other children in the environment of the DLC that she started to emerge as a classroom leader. There was a fire drill at school and Thalia was saying, "I'm not scared," and telling some of her classmates, "don't be scared" as everyone walked outside.

Thalia got excited when Lorena told her that she was going to have her picture taken in school and that she was going to wear a beautiful dress. Thalia smiled happily for her picture. Another classmate was scared and she started to cry when it was her turn to have her picture taken. It was Thalia who comforted her friend and got her to smile for the picture. The teacher remarked to Lorena that everyone at the DLC was proud of Thalia at these moments.

Thalia acted similarly one day at the park. Thalia approached another child to play by nicely asking what was her name. Thalia was telling her new playmate after a couple of minutes to not be scared of the sliding board and to follow her as she slid down.

Thalia enthusiastically passed out the Easter eggs that Lorena sent to school for her classmates and teachers. Thalia greeted each child, with only a little encouragement needed, by saying, "Happy Easter, this is for you." Thalia was equally excited to show off her

Easter dress and the white shoes that Lorena recently bought for her. Thalia was complimented many times at school that day, which she loved.

Easter Sunday was spent at Artie and Vera's house. Thalia got to see and play with Lisa and Tricia. There was an Easter egg hunt in the backyard. Thalia excitingly went around and found the Easter eggs that were hidden for her. John and his wife, Amy, brought their dog, Molly, whom Thalia loved chasing around the backyard all afternoon. That Easter was sixteen months after Lisa's grandmother's birthday party and eight months after the summer that she completed her daily therapy sessions with Thalia. Lisa was seeing a different child. Lisa, who had an understanding of the gravity of the situation, had a true appreciation for how well Thalia was doing. Lisa could have cried at the birthday party because she was filled with sorrow and concern for Thalia. Lisa could now have been brought to tears because she was filled with happiness.

Spending time with her cousins continued to be a big part of Thalia's childhood. Janet's children, Deanna and Daria, and Lorena's older sister, Marisie, and her children, Joey and Klarissa, frequently came to the house to play with Thalia. Uby often visited from college. Uby was relieved to see that Thaila was acting like a typical child. Uby even picked up on Thalia's competitive instincts. Thalia was always trying to go faster than her cousins when they were riding bikes. Lorena's cousin, Cecilia, would take Thalia to an amusement park in the area where she would ride the carousel and go roller skating. Cecilia often took Thalia to Chuck E' Cheese for a day out. Sunday trips to Donnie's parent's house for dinner allowed them and great-grandma Morsillo to spend time with Thalia. Donnie and Janet met at their parents' house on Halloween so that the kids could go trick-or-treating together. Donnie and Janet's families would go apple-picking together in the autumn.

Thalia could have more frequent trips to the park near her house with her cousins when the weather warmed in the spring. A family trip to the circus that spring included Deanna and Daria, Donnie's parents, and great-grandma Morsillo. Thalia especially enjoyed seeing the tigers and the elephants in the circus. Donnie and Lorena took Thalia to Florida to visit his grandparents, Barbara's mother and father. Thalia got to swim and go to the zoo during that trip. Donnie and Lorena also took Thalia to St. Louis to watch Donnie's favorite baseball team, the Cardinals, play a game.

The third pediatric neurologist who evaluated Thalia saw considerable progress at an appointment with her in May 2001. Lorena informed the doctor that Thalia's communication skills greatly improved. Lorena explained that Thalia was very sociable and that she was consistently interacting well with other children. Lorena indicated that Thalia was often initiating conversations. She also told the doctor that Thalia was no longer apprehensive about asking other children to play with her.

The doctor noticed that Thalia was able to speak in three and four-word sentences. Her speech was sometimes difficult to understand in this evaluation. The doctor saw that Thalia recognized more numbers and letters. The doctor became aware of Thalia's issues with recall when he asked her what she ate at her last meal and she had difficulty remembering. The doctor examined Thalia's mental capabilities as part of the evaluation. Thalia performed well on a draw-a-person test. She identified an age-appropriate number of body parts. Thalia was able to draw a circle and a cross when she had to complete that task. The doctor stated at the conclusion of the examination that Thalia should, "stand a good chance," of attending a traditional elementary school for kindergarten. Thalia still had one more year of schooling at the DLC.

CHAPTER 16

T HALIA SEAMLESSLY FELL BACK INTO THE ROUTINE OF THE school day as she started her second year at the DLC. Thalia's learning programs at the beginning of the year mainly focused on her counting to higher numbers and distinguishing between concepts. She worked on understanding the difference between top, middle, or bottom, before or after, and more or less.

Lorena was again encouraged by the DLC teachers to offer details about Thalia's activities when writing in the daily journal so that they could continue to test and improve her recall. The teachers were using the information from the daily journal to engage in more extensive conversations with Thalia. The teachers at the DLC were able to talk to Thalia about her new bike, the movies that she watched, especially her loving *The Little Mermaid*, and how the family celebrated Donnie's birthday. Thalia went to the play telephone several times during the school day in September to pretend to call her father and wish him a happy birthday.

Thalia had to spend the first couple of weeks of the school year in an air cast after tearing a ligament and spraining her foot. Thalia resumed swimming lessons on Saturday once the air cast was removed. Lorena saw a notice for a free trial for a gymnastics class. Thalia went and enjoyed it. Lorena signed up Thalia for a once-a-week gymnastics class that was held on Wednesday. The teachers at the DLC would hear all about swimming and gymnastics classes from Thalia.

One important continued communication improvement was Thalia expressing her wants and needs. Thalia was more often asking for the items that she desired. Thalia was able to tell Lorena what clothes she wanted to wear to school or how she wanted to have her hair brushed. When Lorena had Thalia try on a dinosaur costume for Halloween in 2001, Thalia said to her, "mommy, I don't want to be a dinosaur. I want to be a beautiful ballerina." Thalia was thrilled to tell her teacher and the speech therapist about her Halloween costume choice the next day at school. Thalia's teachers were pleased with this type of expressive communication. It served as the latest sign of her development.

As the educational learning programs were producing positive outcomes, Lorena wanted to ensure that Thalia was listening and paying attention in all aspects of her classroom behavior. A system was set up where Thalia would get a happy face or a sad face if she had a good day or a bad day of listening and following directions at school. If Thalia received a happy face or a sad face became part of the daily journal reporting. Lorena did not have to wait to read the daily journal as Thalia would immediately and proudly tell Lorena when she got home from work if she received a happy face. Thalia knew that her mother was going to reward her with a lollipop or a chocolate chip cookie. There would not be a reward from Lorena when Thalia received a sad face. Thalia would tell her mother, "I'll try again tomorrow to get a happy face."

Thalia received a sad face if she did not follow directions during group time, for example. A teacher might ask Thalia if she understood what needed to be done to complete a certain task. Thalia would respond with the appropriate instructions, but she still might refuse to do that task. The children were to receive a large Halloween cookie as a special snack one afternoon in school. The children were told to raise their hands to receive the cookie. All of the other children raised their hands. Thalia did not comply with this easy instruction. The teacher asked Thalia if she wanted a cookie, to which Thalia responded, "yes." The teacher again told Thalia that she needed to raise her hand to receive the cookie. Thalia then replied, "no."

Refusal to do a simple request, such as raising your hand, is an act of non-compliance. As it is a challenge for anyone conducting an examination to determine a child's behavior condition, the teachers had to figure out when a child does not complete a task if he or she is unable or unwilling. Both can be manifestations of a learning and behavior disability.

The question of being unable or unwilling emerged for Thalia during this time period in speech therapy sessions as well. The speech therapist was experiencing instances when Thalia did not want to talk or answer any questions. Thalia was not making much of an effort during the speech therapy sessions. This behavior was different than how Thalia normally acted in speech therapy sessions, where she routinely tried her best. The speech therapist was struggling to determine if Thalia was having difficulty with the lesson or if she just did not want to do the work on that particular day. The speech therapist worked with Thalia for over a year, but this dilemma persisted. Thalia started to receive a sad face if she did not actively participate during speech therapy. The therapist hoped that would motivate Thalia to improve her behavior.

The teachers were soon finding out that Thalia did not care if she received a sad face. Thalia would say to her teachers, "mommy won't be sad." Just the opposite, Lorena always told Thalia that she was upset when she did not receive a happy face at school. The DLC teachers decided to alter Thalia's happy or sad face plan to make it a group-oriented reward. All of the children were to receive a happy face for good listening and following directions at the end of the school day. The hope was that if the other children were receiving a happy face, but Thalia was not, she might start to care and be motivated to behave better. This strategy produced inconsistent results.

It was determined by the teachers that the happy and sad face system was no longer enough of a reinforcer to entice Thalia to listen and follow directions. A new motivating reward needs to be created and introduced when the reinforcer loses its appeal to a child. The teachers thought of a new reward incentive plan after a group session in which Thalia was not behaving properly. A special box of toys that the teachers knew Thalia enjoyed playing with was put together. Opportunities were created where Thalia would earn a star if she listened and followed the teachers' directions. Thalia would get to play with a toy from the special box for two minutes when she reached the required number of stars. Thalia would start to get put in time-out if she continued to not listen to instructions.

Thalia earned a special toy box reward in only one of the three opportunities that she was given on the first day of the new system. Thalia, however, quickly caught on to the incentive program and within a few days she was consistently earning her special toy box play reward for all three opportunities that were presented. The teachers would add new toys to the box, for which

Thalia would get more motivated to behave well. This improved behavior carried over to Thalia once again having productive speech therapy sessions.

Lorena incorporated reinforcement techniques for Thalia's behavior in other settings. There were a couple of occasions at gymnastics class where the instructor had to repeatedly say to Thalia, "listen to me." Thalia was eager to do certain activities, especially going on the balance beam. Her excitement led her to start to walk on the balance beam before she received permission.

Lorena was clear before one class in telling Thalia that she had to listen to the gymnastics instructor. Thalia began to get teary-eyed. Lorena prepared Thalia that she was going to get a chocolate chip cookie if she listened to the instructor in gymnastics class. Thalia listened perfectly that week. She patiently waited for the instructor to tell her when she could get on the balance beam. The instructor told Thalia that he was happy with her listening. Thalia received a stamp on her hand at the end of the class that said, "I go to gymnastics." Thalia, of course, reminded her mother about receiving her promised cookie.

Lorena sometimes decided to give Thalia only half of a chocolate chip cookie as a reward for a good day of listening at school and save the other half for a good night of listening to her and Donnie at home. This strategy helped if Thalia was hesitant to take a bath, did not want to get dressed, or go to bed. Lorena not permitting Thalia to watch a movie if she did not properly behave was another strategy.

Thalia had a tendency of becoming upset and then frustrated when doing a puzzle or something that she could not quickly figure out. Donnie and Lorena created a system of a time-out chair that they would have Thalia sit in for two minutes to calm down before returning to the activity.

These strategies were not always effective. Lorena wrote to the DLC teachers after consecutive days where Thalia had a tantrum of not listening and acting out in frustration. Thalia was kicking and hitting as Lorena tried to put her in her room. The gymnastics instructor mentioned that same week that Thalia did not listen during class. Lorena asked in her note to the teachers about any ideas to try to help with Thalia's behavior. Lorena indicated that she did not want Thalia to get away with that kind of behavior. The offered advice to Donnie and Lorena was to try to ignore Thalia's crying tantrums, expecting that they would soon end.

Donnie and Lorena had to figure out if any of Thalia's behaviors were caused by her disability, if these actions were attributed to her misunderstanding of a situation, or just the actions of a typical four-year-old child. One example occurred when Lorena took Thalia's Christmas dress to the cleaners in anticipation of her wearing it on the holiday. Thalia got upset as Lorena handed the dress over to the clerk. Thalia kept saying, "it is my dress, not the lady." The clerk took Thalia by the hand and tried to explain to her that she was going to make the dress clean. The clerk told Thalia not to be upset.

Donnie and Lorena were united in not merely giving in to Thalia and letting her have anything that she wanted. They were comfortable with leaving an amusement park or a store if Thalia was not listening. Donnie and Lorena always remained firm, even when one of Thalia's aunts was trying to give a treat of candy or soda to their niece. One of the aunts might say, "how could you say no to her?" Donnie or Lorena reminded their sister that it is not going to be as cute when she gets older and it turns into a bigger behavior issue. Donnie and Lorena decided that Thalia would be disciplined when necessary. Her learning disability was not an excuse for unacceptable behavior.

CHAPTER 17

T HALIA HAD A PEDIATRIC NEUROLOGIST APPOINTMENT ON
December 26, 2001. This evaluation was with the second
doctor who examined her twenty months prior. Lorena informed
the doctor that Thalia spent the summer after her previous evaluation receiving applied behavior analysis therapy with Lisa and that
she was in her second year attending the DLC. Lorena described
Thalia's schooling as effective. Lorena highlighted that Thalia
improved her speech and language skills. Lorena explained that
Thalia had a greater ability to socialize with other children. Lorena
indicated that Thalia was more interactive in playing with her
peers and that she was courteous during these encounters. Lorena
offered an example of Thalia taking turns when participating in
activities with her classmates. Thalia's playing with dolls and her
completing larger number-piece puzzles that did not exist when the
doctor last evaluated her were consistently occurring at an age-appropriate level. Lorena also mentioned that Thalia was enrolled in

swimming and gymnastics classes, independent of her attending school at the DLC.

The doctor was able to easily get and maintain Thalia's attention during the examination. The doctor immediately noticed that Thalia was not making any self-stimulating hand gestures. Thalia's speech was clear. Thalia had improved eye contact, but she tended to avert her eyes briefly when the doctor asked her a question and she began to answer. Thalia accurately responded to the doctor's straightforward questions. The doctor asked Thalia, "are you a boy?" Thalia responded, "no, I am a girl." The doctor asked, "is mommy a boy?" Thalia responded, "no, mommy is a woman." The doctor asked Thalia if, "daddy wears a dress," to which Thalia stated, "no, he wears pants."

The doctor asked Thalia questions about the Barbie doll that she was holding. The doll had long hair. The doctor questioned Thalia if the doll's hair was short. Thalia told him, "no, curly." The doctor continued, "is her hair short or long?" Thalia correctly said, "long." The doctor finally asked about the doll, "is she ugly?" Thalia said, "no, she is great."

Thalia was able to identify the names of common shapes. She correctly pointed out a square, rectangle, and triangle. She identified capital letters. She got slightly confused only when trying to distinguish between an O and a Q. The doctor found that Thalia was not as often repeating her language. Thalia asked the doctor, "what happened to your nose?" After the doctor told her that it was red from frequently using tissues in the winter, Thalia did repeat the question a few minutes later. Thalia's repeating the question was an indication of her difficulty with recall.

The conclusion of the assessment was that Thalia was much improved from her previous visit. The diagnosis was still Pervasive Developmental Disorder/Autism. The doctor felt that there were lingering features of sub-optimal eye contact, getting stuck on a word or thought, and instances of repeating words and phrases that were not relevant. The doctor recommended that Thalia continue to be monitored by teachers and therapists who have a specialization in working with children with autism. The doctor believed that this type of education was necessary to continue her progress and not have her revert to engaging in any self-stimulating behaviors.

One of the general objectives when working with children diagnosed on the autism spectrum is to create structure. An adjustment to a child's behavior routine or environmental familiarity could produce anxiety. Structure was disrupted for Thalia in January 2002, when the DLC moved to a new location. The teachers did lessons with the children before Christmas break to try to make them feel more comfortable with the move. The new school building was located in Union, a few blocks from Donnie and Lorena's house. Thalia would have a shorter bus ride to school. Thalia adapted nicely to the new school. She was happy in her classroom. She particularly liked being able to pick out the color of her lunch tray.

Thalia continued to perform well with her schoolwork. On January 28, 2002, the speech therapist introduced Thalia to a learning program and wrote to Lorena that, "she is catching on very fast." Thalia would become pleased with herself when she did well with writing the letters of the alphabet or drawing a picture that she started to ask her teachers if she could take that work home to show her parents.

Learning programs remained focused on distinguishing concepts. Thalia had some initial difficulty differentiating between above and below. It also took Thalia some time to learn to sequence first, next, and last. More advanced learning programs were implemented. An asking questions program was introduced where the teacher would hold a picture hidden from Thalia's view. Thalia had to ask the teacher questions about the picture to help her guess the answer. This program was used with Thalia having to figure out which animal, vehicle, or piece of clothing was in the picture. Thalia might ask in the guess the animal identification program questions, such as "what color is the animal?" Or, "where does it live?" Questions for the clothing identification program could be, "who wears it?" And, "what is the weather outside?" Questions for the vehicle identification program might include, "how many wheels does it have?"

Identification learning programs were done with Thalia having to pair which like-objects go together and her explaining why they are similar. Listening was worked on by reading to Thalia and having her answer questions about the story. Thalia's ability to listen, stay focused, and respond to "Wh" questions of who, what, where, when, and why about details of the story were the learning objectives of this exercise. Thalia was becoming more interested in books during play breaks, with the Berenstain Bears among her favorites. Her handwriting was improving. Thalia was starting to get exposed to computers as well at the DLC. Donnie bought Thalia a leap pad that she loved playing with at home.

Socially, Thalia continued to appropriately take turns with other students during activities. Thalia was comfortable making suggestions in class. She named the weather bear that was used during the morning group sessions where they learned about the seasons and dressed the bear for that day's weather. Thalia suggested being bears for races during gym class when the students were asked to pretend to be an animal. Thalia volunteered in gym class on one occasion to demonstrate how to run the obstacle course for her classmates. Thalia often served as the line leader when the children walked back to the classroom. The teacher commented to Lorena that Thalia, "shows a good example to the rest of the class."

Thalia's experience at the DLC went well throughout the spring. The teachers found Thalia to be confident in her work and her interactions with the other students. A comment that was becoming typical from the speech therapist was noted on March 26, "Thalia did fantastic work today in speech. She recalled everything you wrote about without prompting and provided additional information. She did great on all of her programs." Another teacher commented in the daily journal on April 22, "Thalia is doing such a nice job with her new programs, especially sight words. She is a very eager learner with so much interest – it's terrific."

Meanwhile, as there were only a couple of months left in the school year, decisions had to be made about Thalia's schooling in September. It needed to be determined if Thalia would remain in a specialized school for kindergarten. Would Thalia be placed in a general education or a special education classroom if she was to return to an in-district school? Considerations about the level of special education support services that she would receive were also going to be discussed.

CHAPTER 18

MUCH HAD BEEN ASKED OF THALIA SINCE LISA BEGAN therapy sessions with her in the summer before she turned three years old. Thalia was in a full-day, year-round school starting in September of that year, with Lorena working with her on most nights. Thalia was at that pace for more than two years by the time she finished her second year of school at the DLC.

All of the teachers who were with Thalia every day were in agreement that she made significant progress in the individualized, structured setting of the DLC. Donnie, Lorena, and Lisa understood that despite all of the consistent and considerable improvement that this was not a time to think that Thalia had completely overcome her disability. They knew that Thalia needed to have the proper education plan for her to develop and thrive. The challenge was to sustain the learning and social behavior growth that she achieved in a new school environment. This was at the forefront of how Donnie and Lorena were approaching the important decisions that were to be made about Thalia's kindergarten placement.

The planning for Thalia's kindergarten year that would commence in September 2002, a couple of weeks after her fifth birthday, began in earnest eight months earlier. The information gathered to make the decisions about Thalia's proper classroom placement was extensive.

An evaluation by another pediatric neurologist was requested by the school district, although Thalia recently had an examination in December 2001. On January 10, 2002, Thalia was examined by the first pediatric neurologist who saw her in April 2000. This was the doctor who offered the bleakest outlook about Thalia's future. Thalia was happy and smiling throughout this evaluation. She showed no signs of distress. Thalia was attentive and cooperative on all of the doctor's requests. Thalia was able to follow the doctor's one and two-step directions without any difficulty. The doctor found Thalia to have improved eye contact. She did not display any acts of self-stimulation.

It was noted that Thalia demonstrated imagination and that she was often engaging in pretend play. It was reported to the doctor that Thalia could communicate her wants and needs. Thalia did speak some words that the doctor found difficult to understand during the evaluation. It was pointed out to the doctor that Thalia struggled with recall. She would remember pieces of information about an activity that she did, but not all of the details. The doctor was informed that prompts and reminders were used to help Thalia recall all of the information about an activity. It was conveyed to the doctor that improving Thalia's recall was an emphasis of her learning.

Whereas twenty-one months earlier Thalia had five of the twelve features on an autism screening form that Lorena filled out, only two of those features remained by the time of this evaluation: inconsistent eye contact and repetition of language. The doctor concluded after the evaluation that the majority of symptoms related to being on the autism spectrum were not present. Some signs of carry-over features of the disability existed. The doctor's overall impression was, "Pervasive Developmental Disorder with significant improvement." The doctor indicated that Thalia was considered to be at risk for attention deficit disorder and hyperactivity, along with a risk for learning disabilities.

The doctor said that Thalia could function in a traditional classroom setting, but it was likely that assistance would be needed to help her stay focused in school. The doctor wrote in the report of Thalia's evaluation, "overall, she has done very well and has come a long way." The doctor's recommendation was for an educational placement as per the child study team.

An IEP meeting was also held on January 10, between Lorena, Lisa, Denise, Thalia's teacher at the DLC, and two representatives from the Union school district. It was the first time in a year that the child study team formally met to discuss Thalia's case. There were no issues with her schooling at the DLC, making additional meetings not necessary.

The IEP meeting in January 2002, had two purposes. The first purpose was to discuss Thalia's academic progress. Any adjustments that needed to be made about the remainder of her school year would be done at this time. Written assessments of Thalia's academic performance by her teacher and the speech therapist from the DLC were provided to the child study team prior to the meeting. Thalia's ability to distinguish between top, middle, and bottom when given a stack of items and her ability to answer, "yes," or, "no," when she was asked questions that started with, "do you," and, "did you" were among the highlights mentioned. It was documented that Thalia could copy the drawings of a snowman and a flower and write her first and last name in capital letters within a one-inch block when given a model.

It was easily agreed by Lorena and the child study team that Thalia would continue with the applied behavior analysis teaching method. Thalia was to receive individual speech and language therapy three times per week for thirty minutes. These decisions were expected due to Thalia's progress and there being only a few months remaining in the school year.

The second, more meaningful, purpose of the January 2002, IEP meeting was to begin the discussions about Thalia's kindergarten education plan. The overall objective was formally written as, "the child study team evaluation will determine Thalia's continued eligibility for special education and appropriate programming to meet Thalia's unique educational needs."

The outcome of the January IEP meeting was that Thalia needed to be comprehensively evaluated by the child study team. The final decisions regarding Thalia's classroom placement and special education services for the beginning of the school year in September would be made later in the spring. Separate evaluations were performed by three different members of the child study team to assess Thalia's education abilities, speech skills, and psychological demeanor.

The education evaluation occurred on January 18. The evaluation included an interview with Thalia's teacher at the DLC and a classroom observation. A school administrator would call Donnie and Lorena to inform them when Thalia was going to be tested. The child study team wanted Donnie and Lorena to make sure that Thalia got a good night's sleep so that she could adequately follow the test instructions and perform her best. Thalia would have a look of exhaustion on her face at the end of her long day of testing. It was a challenging day for Lorena as well. All Lorena could think about was if Thalia was struggling. It was a nauseating feeling. Lorena hated to see that her daughter had to go through these extensive procedures.

A member of the child study team interviewed Thalia's teacher at the DLC. The teacher described Thalia's strengths as acting very social, communicating with spontaneous language, having strong gross and fine motor skills, and that her daily living skills were age appropriate. There were signs of progress in reading, language skills, and cognitive development. Thalia could count and recognize most shapes. The teacher identified Thalia's weaknesses as having a limited attention span and auditory processing problems that made it difficult when she tried to absorb too much information or she had to follow too many directions. There were concerns about Thalia's comprehension skills.

Thalia demonstrated many abilities during the classroom observation. She showed an understanding of some differentiation concepts by being able to place a toy under, over, behind, and next to another object when she was asked. Thalia communicated with her teacher in a clear and understandable voice. Thalia maintained her focus in completing an exercise where she wrote the letters of the alphabet while she was talking to the teacher. Thalia then said that she wanted to color. The teacher asked Thalia to do one more worksheet. Thalia started to complete the worksheet, but she stated, "I think I'm getting tired." Thalia finished the worksheet quickly to just be done with that task.

The child study team examiner witnessed Thalia displaying language that was spontaneous, continuous, and of a social nature in the classroom. Thalia's behavior confirmed what the teacher reported in their interview. It was observed that Thalia interacted well with the other children at school and that she was well-liked by her peers. Thalia was seen engaging in pretend play, seeking other children to play with her, and having conversations with them as they played. Thalia's playing with dolls was witnessed and considered to be appropriate.

Thalia was tested on her reading skills. These tests were conducted with the assistance of Thalia's teacher. Thalia was at ease and comfortable throughout this testing. She was attentive to the tasks. Thalia was talking during this portion of the evaluation, but it was not always relevant to the subject. Thalia identified isolated letters and words. She was able to trace, copy, and write letters. These results indicated that Thalia had some strength in reading readiness. Thalia responded too quickly to the directions on some parts of the test. Thalia was not able to understand a question at times. She offered no response when she found a question difficult.

Thalia was asked to listen to a sequence of audio-recorded instructions and point to various objects in a picture. Thalia was able to successfully point to single objects, but she had difficulty when an instruction required her to point to more than one object. Thalia also struggled when she had to respond to identification questions, for example picking out the top of the tallest tree in the picture.

The speech evaluator deemed there to be deficiencies in both Thalia's receptive and expressive communication. The evaluator found substitutions, omissions, and distortions in Thalia's speech during the classroom observation. The speech evaluation results did reveal some of the positive communication skills that Thalia displayed in the education evaluation.

The psychological evaluation was conducted on January 30. The school psychologist performing the examination served as Thalia's child study team case manager. The psychological evaluation was based on an interview with Thalia and a classroom observation. It was reported to the psychologist going into the evaluation that Thalia had conversational skills where she was able to have a minimum of three communication exchanges with a peer. The psychologist found Thalia to have a friendly demeanor during the interview and classroom observation.

Thalia's DLC teacher was present during the psychologist's interview. The teacher would indicate to the psychologist if she felt that Thalia needed a break. It was evident that Thalia had a good relationship and comfort level with her teacher. Thalia was able to comply with the structure of the interview. She did not appear to be distressed, although this assessment was a significant departure from her daily routine. Thalia's teacher offered her verbal praise and treats were available to replicate the positive reinforcement that she was accustomed.

Thalia demonstrated her complete understanding of the structure of the school day during the psychologist's classroom observation. Thalia was found to be a happy, highly verbal child. Thalia was an active participant during group sessions. She spoke when it was appropriate. She equally displayed knowing to remain quiet when the teachers or other students were talking. Thalia received a star for listening that day.

Thalia properly raised her hand to respond to the teacher's questions during group time. Thalia correctly gave the date when asked. It was Thalia's turn to answer a question about that day's weather. Thalia followed the group-time rules of asking another student to help her decide the answer. Thalia returned to the group and responded, "today is cloudy." The teacher then asked Thalia, "how does it feel outside?" Thalia responded, "cold." The group put the proper clothing on the weather bear that matched that day's weather. Thalia appropriately put a hat on the bear. Thalia repeated the words and she attempted the hand motions as the children sang

"Itsy Bitsy Spider" in another group session activity. Thalia also located her name and she put her picture in the attendance slot.

The psychologist saw Thalia playing in the kitchen area with a doll when she was on a break from a learning session. Thalia lined up pots and pans on a blanket and pretended to stir something in the pot. She pretended to put food on a plate and feed the doll as it was sitting in a chair. Thalia picked up the doll and put it in a carriage before placing it in a crib. Thalia was occasionally guided by her teacher with verbal cues during this period of play.

The psychologist observed Thalia receiving an individualized learning program. The psychologist found Thalia to be enthusiastic and responsive during this therapy session. Thalia was able to appropriately respond when she was asked a series of questions: do you have Blue's Clues treats? Do you have two eyes? Do you have two noses? Do you have three feet? Do you ride a bike? Thalia helped her teacher wipe some water that spilled on the table during the therapy session.

The psychologist had Thalia assemble puzzles and copy patterns using blocks. Thalia was tested for her visual learning capabilities. She was able to identify what was missing in a series of pictures. Thalia had to do a matching test where she was presented with objects of different shapes. She got the majority of the matching shapes correct. There were only a couple of shapes that she had difficulty pairing. On those, Thalia selected similar configurations, but she missed one detail that was in the design, leading to her incorrect response. Thalia had trouble following a direction for an exercise where she was to draw the shortest line between two objects.

Thalia was asked questions related to her language skills. Thalia had a hard time defining some words. She was able to correctly respond to only half of the sentence completion requests. Many of these responses were incomplete. The nature of Thalia's mistakes suggested that she understood the questions as her responses were related to the general topic. The psychologist concluded that a verbal-only format of direct questioning was not Thalia's preferred method of responding and learning. Thalia's learning strength was identified as being in visual perception.

There were two guiding thoughts by the child study team about Thalia's kindergarten schooling plan after the evaluations were conducted. First, Thalia still had a diagnosis from a pediatric neurologist that placed her on the autism spectrum. Second, Thalia continued to have delays in her language skills and aspects of her social interactive behavior.

Three members of the child study team met with Lorena, Lisa, and Thalia's teacher from the DLC at the end of March 2002. The simple conclusion of this meeting was that Thalia was indeed ready to transition back to the school district for her education. The result that Thalia would return to the Union school system to attend kindergarten was the expectation of everyone in the decision-making process, including Donnie and Lorena. The DLC benefited Thalia tremendously, but her remaining there beyond the school year was not an option. This was a positive outcome in many ways. Thalia was achieving behaviors at a level where she no longer required a specialized school for children with autism. The child study team felt that Thalia could transition into a traditional elementary school if done properly.

Another very predictable outcome of the evaluation was that Thalia remained eligible for special education support services. An update on her academic skills was provided at the March meeting. It was determined that Thalia was reading at approximately a kindergarten grade level. Language areas in need of development included sight vocabulary, comprehension, and phonics, the correlating of sounds with letters or groups of letters that help children learn to read. Thalia's writing and speaking skills were found to be at approximately a kindergarten level.

Thalia's overall math performance was reported at approximately a kindergarten level. Her math strengths were identifying numbers from one through fifty, and sequencing numbers from one through twenty. Thalia could match and organize items into a requested set of numbers, such as if she was asked to organize four pictures of animals. She could recognize some coins. Thalia's academic performance in math problem solving was considered at a pre-kindergarten grade level.

It was determined that Thalia handled age-appropriate tasks independently. She was considered to be capable of adapting to new settings and environments. Thalia was described as a highly motivated student who was curious. She closely followed the rules of the school. It was documented that the use of positive reinforcement was the most successful way to maintain Thalia's interest and effort.

The benefits of Thalia being placed in a general education, mainstream classroom were considered. The most notable benefit was that it would allow Thalia to be in a classroom with non-disabled peer role models. Thalia would also receive the entirety of the grade level academic curriculum in a general education classroom. Those reasons were countered by pointing out that the type of learning that Thalia was receiving at the DLC with individualized and small group approaches was providing the focus that enabled her to achieve substantial progress. Thalia's specialized instruction and support assisted in her language development and her improved communication behaviors. It was pointed out that the DLC provided the structure in the school day that was needed to develop Thalia's social skills. A general education classroom could provide significant distractions that would impact her growth in both academics and socialization.

It was decided that the characteristics related to Thalia's Pervasive Developmental Disorder/Autism diagnosis required that she start the school year in a special education classroom. This classroom would have fewer students. It was noted that the general education kindergarten classroom could not provide the individualized instruction critical for Thalia's success. Thalia would still be exposed to grade level curriculum objectives within the special education classroom. Thalia was going to interact with the children from the general education classroom in non-academic activities.

Thalia was to receive both in-class and out-of-the-classroom speech and language therapy twice per week for thirty minutes. Thalia would have a one-on-one teacher's aide with her every day in all settings. Thalia received bus transportation to school because of her diagnosis. It was believed that these accommodations best enabled Thalia to continue to progress in her speech, language, comprehension, and socialization behavior goals. Donnie and Lorena agreed to this classroom placement and education plan. Lorena signed the IEP on May 29, 2002. Thalia was heading to kindergarten at a traditional elementary school in a special education classroom.

CHAPTER 19

THERE WERE SOME OBVIOUS DIFFERENCES IN HOW THALIA was going to experience school in kindergarten. Thalia was no longer being taught using the applied behavior analysis method. Thalia was going to receive less one-on-one instruction, even though her initial kindergarten placement was in a special education classroom. She would also not receive constant reinforcement rewards.

The primary purpose of Thalia's teacher's aide was to assist her with starting assignments and making sure that she understood all of the directions. The aide might repeat or rephrase directions, use visual aids, or give a subtle prompt to alert Thalia to pay attention when the teacher was giving an instruction or asking her a question. The aide might make eye contact with Thalia or gently touch her on the forearm or shoulder while pointing to the teacher. The aide would offer Thalia praise and encouragement to keep her motivated in class.

Ideally, the teacher's aide acts in such a way that the other students do not necessarily know which child in the classroom requires assistance. The aide is there to help the assigned child, but can assist any child in the classroom. The aide should not be sitting exclusively next to the assigned child. The stigma for a child of having an individual assistant can be lessened or removed if an aide is moving around the room. Finally, the aide is designed to help only when the child has a question or is struggling. The aide certainly should not do the work for the child. The aide needs to be patient and not become frustrated when the child is having difficulty completing a task.

An IEP meeting was held in September to evaluate Thalia's transition to kindergarten. Lorena and Lisa met with the case manager of the child study team, Thalia's special education classroom teacher, the speech and language specialist who was working with Thalia, and a general education kindergarten teacher. The purpose of this meeting as stated in the IEP document was to, "describe the present levels of performance including how the child's disability affects her involvement and progress in the general education curriculum." The academic assessment was largely based on Thalia's performance in kindergarten, despite it being only a few weeks into the school year.

It was explained to Lorena and Lisa that Thalia was reading, writing, and spelling at approximately a kindergarten level. Thalia's performance in math was also considered to be at a kindergarten level. Thalia knew all of the essential colors. She knew most letter sounds. Thalia was able to connect the sounds to words that began with those letters, although her phonics ability was identified as an area in need of improvement.

Other areas in need of improvement noted in the IEP were Thalia's sight vocabulary and comprehension. The teachers wanted

Thalia to improve her proper use of plural words and improve her recall, an area that was of constant emphasis during her two years at the DLC. The teachers felt that Thalia had some strengths in receptive and expressive communication, but that she needed assistance in using words to better describe things in her environment. The teachers wanted Thalia to improve her handwriting and her ability to copy sentences from the board.

Thalia demonstrated strong work habits. She was following two to three-step directions. Thalia's teacher pointed out that she was participating in classroom activities. She performed well in physical education class. Socially, Thalia displayed interactive skills in group play. She was developing friendships with her classmates. Overall, the child study team felt that Thalia was making a good adjustment to kindergarten and her new school.

One point of consideration raised in the September IEP was if Thalia would receive an extended school year for the summer between kindergarten and first grade. It was stated at one point in the IEP that this decision would be made later in the school year. Thalia's academic and social progress would be the factors in that determination. A box was checked at another point in the same IEP document that indicated that Thalia's school year would be only ten months in accordance with the school calendar. Making sure that the family and the child study team are clear on the education plan is something that requires constant vigilance.

Some areas of concern were developing from Donnie and Lorena's perspective, despite the child study team's assessment that Thalia's transition was going well. Thalia was with a larger group of students in the special education kindergarten class than at the DLC. The children in Thalia's class at the DLC were also of similar education and social interaction needs. Many of the children in Thalia's kindergarten class had different special education disabilities, some more behavioral. Thalia was now interested in wanting to play and interact with her classmates. Lorena had a fear that Thalia could easily pick up on some of the other students' more detrimental behaviors. For Lorena, it seemed as if Thalia was being used as the peer role model in this kindergarten social environment.

The greater emerging issue at this early stage of the school year was the possibility of Thalia moving into a general education, mainstream classroom setting. The child study team clearly indicated that this transition was the eventual objective. Thalia was participating only in non-academic activities with her non-disabled peers for the first month of school. The belief at the September meeting was that Thalia needed more time to adjust to her academic subjects before any changes in her educational plan were to be implemented. Donnie and Lorena agreed with this patient approach.

The child study team met again with Lorena and Lisa three weeks later in October. There were not any substantial changes in Thalia's academic progress report. Thalia's strengths and the areas desired for improvement mentioned in the September IEP remained the same. There was one subtle change to Thalia's IEP in that the box for an extended school year was now checked. This offered clarity in indicating that summer school was required. It was reported in the October IEP that Thalia was beginning to raise her hand in class with some prompting. Thalia often responded with the correct answer when she was called on by the teacher.

Thalia's adjustment from the DLC into the special education kindergarten classroom was again thought to be going well according to her teachers. The positive assessment by her teachers was used in making the argument that Thalia was ready for advancement into more mainstream settings. It was a sudden reversal from the sentiment that Thalia, "needed more time to adjust," which was conveyed just one month earlier. Thalia's teachers pointed out that Thalia appeared to be socially comfortable when she interacted with the students in the general education kindergarten class during playtime. The child study team decided to have Thalia participate in music class with the general education kindergarten class as the next step. There were also discussions about Thalia having other subjects in the general education classroom.

Lorena forcefully raised questions about Thalia's movement into mainstream classroom settings at the October IEP meeting. Lorena particularly wanted to know about the group dynamics that Thalia would be exposed. Thalia primarily interacted with one teacher who presented academic programs that were tailored to her learning needs in the special education program. Thalia would lose that more individualized approach in the general education classroom. Lorena wondered if the child study team was being too aggressive in attempting to mainstream Thalia.

By December 2002, the dominant issue of the IEP meetings was the amount of time in the general education classroom that Thalia would receive. The child study team again indicated its desire to move Thalia into mainstream settings. Lorena and Lisa argued that this was a critical time period in Thalia's development. They sincerely felt that it seemed like too big of a jump for Thalia. Lorena and Lisa implored the child study team that Thalia's learning environment was essential to her progress. They believed that support services were still very much needed for both education and social behavior development, or Thalia could easily regress. From Lorena's perspective, it appeared that the child study team's measurement of Thalia's success was based solely on her being mainstreamed.

Lorena would ask the child study team for the maximum

services in the quest for special education support. For example, Lorena tried to get Thalia to receive speech therapy five days a week. Lorena hoped that a compromise could be reached and that Thalia would receive one additional day of speech therapy. This tactic did not bring any results. Lorena requested additional IEP meetings to try to convince the child study team that Thalia needed more support. Nothing worked and the suggestions from Lorena and Lisa were generally not acted upon.

Lorena and Lisa felt that they had a compelling case in their pleas to the child study team. They knew Thalia's behavior tendencies and her education history. They could point to what worked for Thalia in the past. Lorena and Lisa thought that their guiding the child study team would be welcomed. The child study team continued to make decisions as if Lorena and Lisa offered no value in the process. Lorena and Lisa became frustrated with not being listened to and feeling that their input was not needed.

The child study team thought that Thalia was receiving the support services that she needed. The child study team also believed that Thalia would adapt well to the mainstream classroom setting. Lorena and Lisa soon had to take the minimalist position of arguing for the status quo of Thalia's time spent in the special education and the general education classroom. It was stated in the December IEP that Thalia, "will be mainstreamed for reading and language arts" rather than having her maintain the same classroom-type time distribution.

CHAPTER 20

Lisa's experience as a teacher motivated her to learn more about working with children with disabilities. Lisa enrolled in graduate school at New Jersey City University. She earned a master's degree in special education in May 2000. Teaching during the day and attending class at night took a great amount of time and effort, but Lisa enjoyed getting exposed to different teaching strategies and hearing about the experiences of the other students in the master's program.

Lisa was especially becoming infatuated with teaching using the principles of applied behavior analysis that she learned at the DLC. She implemented this approach in teaching her class in the Clinton school district. Lisa could point to her experience as evidence that applied behavior analysis was effective in improving the behaviors of some of the children with autism. Thalia being one of her favorite examples.

Two of Lisa's friends at the DLC told her about a master's

degree program in behavior disorders that they were enrolled in at Columbia University's Teacher's College. The program had a narrow focus on training its graduate students how to teach children using the principles of applied behavior analysis. Lisa thought that it was an amazing opportunity to advance her knowledge. She knew that she would love being around other students in the program who shared her passion for the subject. It was a one-year program so it appeared manageable in terms of the number of courses and the overall commitment to earn the degree.

Lisa was particularly drawn to the practical experience component of the program. Columbia University contracted with some school districts in New York. The graduate students would work in the classrooms dedicated to children on the autism spectrum and implement the applied behavior analysis principles that they were learning in their own classes. This working requirement during the day and her taking classes at night, along with studying and completing assignments, meant that Lisa had to step away from her job. Leaving her teaching position at Clinton was a risk for Lisa. Lisa, however, felt that she might not ever end up attending Columbia if she did not enroll in the program at this time. Lisa applied for the program and she was accepted to start in the fall 2001 semester.

Lisa thought that she had a strong knowledge of teaching children with autism and using applied behavior analysis in a practical setting. She had more than six years of classroom experience. Lisa quickly became amazed at how much she was learning in Columbia's program. Lisa was being taught the science behind why teaching using these principles was effective.

An overall theme of the Columbia program was to develop teaching skills to enable and accelerate learning for all children. The Columbia program put a great amount of attention on a child's language development. Communication skills were identified as a primary reason for the learning difficulties of many children, especially those on the autism spectrum. More than recognizing the general symptomatic characteristics of a child with autism, Lisa learned to better identify a child's missing communication and behavior capabilities.

The use of performance data to indicate if a child was responding to a learning program was another core focus of the Columbia program. Lisa learned to interpret the data to provide the programs that addressed a child's identified deficiencies. Lisa was getting exposed to the research that documented which programs were successful. She became aware of more learning programs than what she was familiar with while working at the DLC. This was especially helpful knowing that children learn and respond differently based on the learning program. Lisa was becoming better prepared to quickly switch if one program was not working to improve a child's skill. The quest was to find the most appropriate learning program for each child's language and behavior development needs. Lisa was drilled that the process from observation and skill identification, to learning program implementation, to collecting and using data was about getting children to perform behaviors that they were not capable of doing prior.

Lisa was expanding her knowledge of techniques to help children learn through observation, peer role modeling, and rewarding behavior. The Columbia program discussed how to motivate children through positive reinforcement. The program also introduced Lisa how to evolve from using reinforcer rewards to getting a child to consistently do appropriate behaviors out of desire, such as having a conversation or a social peer interaction being the source of a rewarding experience. The program was intended to train graduate students in how to teach children to be motivated self-learners.

The courses in the Columbia program provided training in

classroom management, curriculum development, and a variety of effective teaching practices. Lisa was learning about research methods, data recording specifically for applied behavior analysis, working with families of children with autism, and professional and ethical issues in behavior analysis treatment. Lisa rotated to different schools to work with autistic children of different ages and different skill levels for the practical teaching component of the program. The entire experience was making Lisa better informed and more skilled at helping children learn. Lisa was thrilled with the Columbia program and the people that she was meeting. It exceeded all of her expectations.

Lisa wished that she had some of this knowledge when she had her therapy sessions with Thalia, although she believed that Thalia made substantial progress with the learning programs that were used in the summer when they worked together. Lisa was able to bring what she was learning through Columbia's program into Thalia's IEP meetings with the Union child study team. Lisa's worries about the teaching methods being used during Thalia's kindergarten school year emanated from the greater understanding of educating children on the autism spectrum that she acquired at Columbia.

Lisa completed her second master's degree in May 2002. The Columbia program presented her with an incredible opportunity upon graduation. Columbia University contracted to work with schools in Ireland to develop programs for children with autism. Lisa was asked to go to Dublin to help establish the programs. Lisa would train the teachers in the principles of applied behavior analysis and supervise these newly set up classrooms. Lisa traveled to Dublin throughout the summer and the fall. She and Rich would then spend six months in Dublin starting in January 2003.

The IEP meeting in December 2002 was the last that Lisa

attended with the Union child study team. Lisa tried her best to keep up with how Thalia was performing in school. International communication in 2003 was more difficult than with present-day technologies. Lisa mostly communicated with Lorena, and her other family and friends, through email. Lisa had to go to a local Internet café that charged by the minute for computer usage to respond to her email messages. Lisa learned from Lorena that Thalia's situation with the Union school district was not improving.

CHAPTER 21

Afree, appropriate public education as required by federal law and administered by the state and local district is a foundational commitment made to every student. The term, "appropriate," however, is ambiguous. What is deemed appropriate can be a point of contention between a school district and a family in the context of the special education support services that are provided to a child. The design of the IEP process is to develop and agree on an education plan that both sides believe matches the appropriate standard.

The relationship between Lorena and the Union child study team continued to deteriorate as the discrepancy over the amount of time that Thalia would spend in a general education, mainstream classroom remained. It reached the point where one option that Lorena explored and presented to the child study team was Thalia attending an out-of-district school. Lorena went and observed a private school that had a smaller class size and had a teacher's aide present in the classroom. The private school offered individualized instruction for all of the students in the class, from the academically talented to those children with special education needs. Thalia would be at the private school where her social interactions would be with more suitable peer role models while getting her individual academic needs met. It was the type of inclusionary experience that Lorena coveted.

Union school administrators balked at an out-of-district placement. The school district was not about to pay for educational services that it believed it was capable of providing. Lorena continued to want to know exactly what the general education experience would be like for Thalia. For Lorena, while part of her was eager to have Thalia challenged in a mainstream setting, she worried that Thalia might be overwhelmed. Lorena did not want Thalia to get lost when following the class lessons and directions. Lorena feared that Thalia would get frustrated, stop trying in class, and regress if this occurred. Much that Thalia worked to achieve would be lost.

The thoughts of Thalia's teachers continued to serve as the primary evidence that warranted Thalia's further movement into a mainstream classroom for more academic subjects. Thalia's special education teacher described Thalia as, "a pleasure to have in class. She works well in class and play with her peers." The special education teacher added, "Thalia is a very sweet girl. I am happy with her progress." The general education teacher remarked, "Thalia has adjusted nicely to our classroom. At times when we work in large groups, her attention has to be redirected. I am pleased with her progress." There was nothing in either teacher's estimation that justified Thalia not having a more general education experience.

The March 3 IEP provided a detailed overview of all aspects of Thalia's classroom performance. Thalia was thought to be at ease with her teachers. There were no behavior issues in any classroom setting. The teachers pointed out that Thalia willingly followed rules and that she complied with their requests. She eagerly participated in classroom activities. Thalia showed responsibility for her personal belongings. Thalia was routinely sharing, taking turns, and using good manners during social interactions with the other children. Thalia was described as an asset to the classroom.

Thalia developed good study habits. Thalia used classroom materials appropriately and she worked neatly. Thalia was found to be task-oriented and organized. Thalia was responding appropriately to the teacher's and the aide's prompts and reminders on the occasions when she did become distracted.

Thalia started having reading and language arts with the general education class in December. Reading and language arts was the first core academic subject that Thalia participated in the mainstream classroom. How Thalia handled that subject was used in the debate over her shifting to general education settings for more academic subjects.

Thalia was reading at grade level. She started to show a greater interest in books and stories. Thalia was developing a sight vocabulary and she was acquiring phonics skills, two areas identified as wanting to see improvement at the beginning of the school year. It was now indicated that Thalia showed a greater interest in phonics. Thalia knew the letter sounds that she was taught and she was able to identify those letter sounds in words. The March 3 IEP reported that Thalia made a good transition in reading and language arts in the general education classroom.

There were skills noted as needing improvement. The teacher wanted Thalia to develop an ability to express her thoughts and ideas. Thalia was better at verbal communication than writing. Thalia required assistance from her aide in getting started on writing assignments. Thalia found it challenging to come up with an idea to write about. She then needed to develop her language skills to put those ideas into an organized written sentence. Thalia was also having difficulty with the use of past tense verbs when writing sentences. It was felt that these deficiencies were not enough to limit her academic plan.

Thalia was developing a vocabulary in science and social studies. Thalia's skill level indicated to her teachers that she could be part of the general education class for both of those subjects. Thalia had some deficiencies in math, but it was expressed in the March IEP that Thalia's teacher could provide any needed assistance. Thalia's math skills were thought to enable her to participate in a mainstream math class within the next two weeks.

Thalia was performing at a satisfactory level in art, music, physical education, and computers. It was also noted in the March IEP that Thalia was demonstrating social skills and that she displayed a sense of humor as she had more interactions with the children in the general education class. It was reported that Thalia enjoyed being with her non-disabled peers. The conclusion in early March from the child study team was that Thalia appeared to be ready to transition into a general education kindergarten class full-time.

Thalia's transition plan into the mainstream classroom was to be conducted in two phases. The first phase was to begin on March 17. Thalia was to arrive at school and go to the special education classroom where she would pick out what she wanted for lunch. At 9:15, Thalia would join the general education class to participate in reading and language arts, math, and either a science or a social studies lesson. Thalia was to return to the special education classroom at 12:15 to eat lunch.

Thalia would remain in the special education classroom for one hour of individual instruction to start the afternoon. Thalia continued to receive speech therapy for thirty minutes, twice per week in an in-class group format and an individual format where she was pulled out of the classroom. It was deemed that Thalia still needed speech therapy to address her language weaknesses. Thalia was to have physical education with the special education class. She was then scheduled to participate in playtime with the general education class. The final period of the day was to have Thalia back in the special education classroom. Thalia's individual teacher's aide would continue to travel with her to the different classrooms. For a child who coveted structure, as Thalia did, this daily school day arrangement seemed ill-conceived. This schedule was the latest major point of contention for Donnie and Lorena with the child study team.

The second phase of Thalia's transition was to occur in early April. The plan was to move Thalia into a complete general education, mainstream experience. A goal was for Thalia to work more independently without any prompts from her aide.

The teachers were steadfast in their belief that the mainstreaming strategies that were implemented up until that point in the school year for Thalia had been effective. They believed that Thalia made significant progress throughout the school year. They thought that Thalia's academic skills matched those of the other children in the classroom. Thalia had not regressed in any areas of her academic performance. There was a slight improvement noted in Thalia's ability to express her thoughts and ideas. The general education teacher commented, "Thalia's gradual transition worked out wonderfully. She works well with the other students and seems to be happy in our class. She is still very easily distracted by her neighbors, but once she is refocused, she successfully completes her tasks."

The teachers and the child study team felt that this progress aligned with the decision to transition Thalia into the mainstream, general education setting full-time. Lorena continued to be skeptical of the child study team's plan. Lorena was also starting to get the impression that Thalia would be completely mainstreamed in first grade, quite possibly with no additional speech and language therapy and without a teacher's aide in the classroom. Lorena was downright frightened by the prospect of Thalia receiving no special education support services. Donnie and Lorena acknowledged that there was some academic progress. They would end up never considering at any point in Thalia's schooling to have her repeat a grade. Donnie and Lorena, however, were uneasy with the direction of Thalia's education plan.

Lisa became convinced after hearing from Lorena that the Union school district was not going to alter its position about Thalia's classroom placement. Lisa knew that the situation reached another moment where she had to give Lorena her blunt opinion. Lisa said to Lorena that if she and Donnie stayed in Union that the only way that they might receive what they believed were the appropriate support services for Thalia would be to sue the school district. Lisa had some familiarity with the litigation process. She was aware of examples where a lawsuit took up a great amount of time, with the child not receiving the support services that were needed, and the parents having the expense of hiring a lawyer.

Lisa offered another thought. She told Lorena, "you should think about moving somewhere else." It was a bold suggestion and one that Lisa would not have made unless she believed it to be necessary. Lisa recommended the Clinton school district, where she previously worked, or the town of Livingston, which she heard had a strong special education program. Lorena told Donnie of Lisa's idea. It was a proposition that was unexpected, but Donnie and Lorena knew that a difference of opinion existed with the child study team. Donnie and Lorena were very doubtful that the problems of Thalia's schooling would be resolved to their satisfaction. They felt that there was no time to waste to see if the Union school district would acquiesce and alter the educational support services for Thalia.

Donnie and Lorena understood that moving to a new house was going to be a greater financial burden. They would have to move to a town where the houses were more expensive. They were almost a decade into paying off the mortgage on their house. Donnie and Lorena thought that Thalia was still young enough in school where she had not made long-time friends and that she was yet to truly become involved in the community's activities. Yes, they took great advantage of living near a park, but the neighborhood where they lived had many older families. Donnie and Lorena believed that the move needed to be done from an educational perspective. They also came to think of it as an opportunity to find a house that could have social neighborhood benefits for Thalia as well. The decision to move ended up being made with little debate. Donnie and Lorena immediately began looking for a new house.

CHAPTER 22

Donnie and Lorena felt that the town of Clinton was too far from where they both worked and from where their parents and sisters lived. Livingston became the focus of their house search. They put in a bid on only one house in Livingston and it was accepted. Thalia was going to be enrolled in first grade in that school district. Donnie and Lorena liked that the house was close to the elementary school that Thalia would attend. The morning routine was going to be Donnie walking his daughter to school.

First grade had Thalia attending her third different school in three years. Donnie and Lorena knew that this type of change could be a challenge for Thalia. They also worried about what their options might be if the Livingston school district did not provide Thalia with the support services that they believed were needed to satisfy all of her educational needs.

Donnie and Lorena were determined to be proactive from the outset in dealing with the Livingston school district. Lorena dropped off all of Thalia's IEP reports and pediatric neurologist evaluations to the Livingston special services office. Thalia had her official diagnosis of Pervasive Developmental Disorder/Autism, which established her eligibility for assistance. The special services office also received the results of educational testing that was done at the end of Thalia's kindergarten school year. Thalia was assessed as having seventy-two of seventy-six grade level language skills and seventy-four of seventy-five grade level math skills.

Lorena wrote a letter to the Livingston director of special services in August, a couple of weeks before the start of the school year. Lorena requested that an evaluation be conducted by the Livingston child study team to determine Thalia's first grade classroom placement. Lorena expressed her concern about the teacher-to-student ratio that Thalia was to receive. Lorena wrote in the letter, "as a parent, I want her transition to be as smooth as possible. I also want her to be academically successful in a new environment and teaching structure."

The Livingston school district decided to first try Thalia in a general education classroom with her own individual teacher's aide. The feeling of the child study team was that Thalia's academic performance supported that conclusion. Thalia was to receive speech therapy in a separate classroom for thirty minutes, twice per week. Thalia would participate in all co-curricular activities with the students from the general education classroom. The benefits of this plan were described as ensuring maximal opportunity for socialization with non-disabled children to create peer role-modeling opportunities. Donnie and Lorena were a bit reluctant to this mainstream approach after Thalia's kindergarten experience. They were assured by the child study team that Thalia would be closely monitored and that adjustments would be made if needed.

Thalia's academic performance and social behavior early in the school year were going to be pivotal in deciding if this plan was going to be altered. The initial academic impression of Thalia by her teacher was that she was reading at grade level. Thalia demonstrated an ability to properly write letters. Thalia was having some difficulty in math. She could write numbers appropriately, but there were concerns about her ability to understand math concepts and apply them to problem-solving. Thalia often had trouble explaining how she arrived at an answer to a math problem. She was rarely participating in class during math lessons.

The main issue that emerged was Thalia's short attention span, a characteristic of her disability. Thalia was regularly getting distracted and it was impeding her learning. Thalia's difficulty maintaining her focus was causing her to miss directions on assignments. She often completed assignments at a slower pace than her classmates because of her inability to focus. Thalia would lose focus by looking at the pictures that were hanging on a wall in the classroom, other children's behavior, any out-of-the-ordinary activity that might occur in the classroom, and her own thoughts. Thalia could easily start daydreaming about something other than her schoolwork. Thalia would sometimes get up from her seat and start to do another activity in the classroom when she lost focus. This might occur in the middle of a lesson or a conversation.

Several typical strategies can be used to help a child stay focused. Thalia would have her desk located close to the teacher in the classroom. Visual prompting and having the directions for an assignment written on the board helped her. Thalia benefited from having directions given to her in small bits and repeated by the aide.

Thalia had some minor social behaviors that caused an issue with her classmates. Perhaps still a bit reflective of her two years at the DLC in a friendly environment, Thalia would express her affection to the other children by hugging them. Some of her classmates were not comfortable with that action. Thalia might tell her classmates when they were doing something wrong, such as if they were talking when they were supposed to be quiet. Her peers did not like that as well.

Thalia was cooperative and an active participant in her speech therapy sessions. One significant difference between Thalia's kindergarten and first grade experience was her being better matched with peers of similar needs in speech therapy. Thalia was more easily brought back into focus on the learning tasks when she became distracted in the speech therapy learning environment. Thalia was also better capable of following assignment directions in this setting.

Improving Thalia's focus during communication interactions was an objective of speech therapy. Thalia could initiate conversations and there was a back-and-forth nature to these interactions. On occasion, what she was talking about would drift from the topic. One of the learning programs used in speech therapy to help Thalia's communication stay on topic and have a logical progression was to get her to sequence and tell picture stories. Thalia was able to correctly sequence four-scene stories and discuss what was occurring in the story. She quickly advanced to sequencing five-scene stories. Thalia also worked throughout the year on answering "Wh" questions and correctly using past tense verbs in speech therapy.

An IEP meeting was held on October 23 between Lorena and five members of the Livingston child study team. Present from the school district were Thalia's general education teacher, speech and language pathologist, a special education teacher, a psychologist, and the school principal. The IEP report contained a lengthy list of the areas that Thalia needed to improve, "self-control, interaction with peers, attentiveness, ability to complete tasks, follow directions, work independently, organization, and participation in class activities." It was declared that the main responsibility of Thalia's aide was to review assignment directions, keep her focused, and to "limit off-task behavior." Classroom observations by members of the child study team confirmed that Thalia required the support of an individual aide, "to maintain academic and behavior expectations."

There were some noted strengths in Thalia's early school year performance. Thalia had a cooperative attitude and she was always courteous in the classroom. Thalia consistently observed school rules. She was thought to have a nice self-image. Thalia showed positive work habits. She always completed her homework assignments on time. She often sought help when needed in the classroom.

By December, Thalia's teacher found her to be adjusting well to the first grade. Thalia was described by her teacher as a very loving girl who was a happy member of the class. Thalia was said to be well-liked by her classmates. The teacher commented that Thalia was, "a pleasure to have in class."

Thalia impressed her teachers by dramatically improving in several areas throughout the school year. Her social development in first grade was considered significant. Whereas Thalia had only one friend in the class in September, she had many friends when the school year ended. Thalia's growth when interacting with her classmates was attributed to her improved communication skills. Thalia became more capable of initiating a conversation. Thalia could now consistently maintain a communication interaction for six exchanges when she was focused. Her word choice was often appropriate for those social interactions. Thalia might have some problems relating her experiences to a conversation. She could better recall those facts with a little prompting.

The social concern for Thalia remained that she could be sensitive at times, which did interfere with some of her peer interactions.

There was also an occasional period of difficulty for Thalia if things did not go her way. Some of these behaviors were typical of any child who had an emotional disposition. They manifested themselves a bit more with Thalia's developmental disorder.

Thalia showed some improvement in math. She started to become eager to participate in math class. She still needed additional individual assistance when solving problems. The teacher worked with Thalia to implement strategies to help her remember some basic math facts. The teacher would sit with Thalia and they would solve math problems together. This extra attention by the teacher was meaningful to Lorena. It was the type of support that she wanted Thalia to receive. The teacher was pleased with Thalia's effort in trying to learn the math concepts and use them to arrive at the correct answers.

Thalia was on grade level for all of her subjects at the end of the school year. The learning activity that she most enjoyed was reading and listening to stories. Thalia was actively contributing during class discussions about the stories that the students were reading. Thalia showed that she could independently finish her reading and language assignments. She only occasionally needed the help of her aide to complete those tasks. Her phonics awareness was improving. Thalia developed reading strategies for when she got to a word that she did not know. Her teacher described Thalia at the end of the school year as, "a wonderful reader."

The teacher suggested that Lorena read with Thalia for ten minutes every night. Lorena constantly read with Thalia. It was more than thirty minutes on most nights. Lorena always encouraged Thalia's love of reading. Lorena would buy many books for Thalia when the book fair was held at school every year. When Thalia got older, Lorena made sure that she brought extra money with her to school for the book fair so that she could buy what she wanted to read.

Lisa accompanied Lorena to the final IEP meeting held in June of Thalia's first grade year. Lisa was immediately thrilled. Lisa was impressed with the special education program. She was also impressed with the knowledge of the child study team when listening to its members explain the education and behavior plan for Thalia. Lisa felt that there were logical reasons for the approaches that the child study team was implementing. Lisa thought that Thalia was getting the support services that she needed in terms of speech and language therapy and peer group interaction. Lisa told Lorena that she did not think that she had to attend future child study team meetings. As Lisa did when Thalia was about to start the DLC, she said to Lorena that Thalia is, "exactly where she needs to be."

It was concluded that Thalia did not need an extended school year in the summer as a regression in her academic skills was not expected. Thalia could attend the school's summer program that was available to all students, but she decided to participate in summer camp at the YMCA.

The plan for the second grade was to keep Thalia in a general education classroom and continue with her having an individual aide. The communication and social behavior progress were significant to the extent that it was decided that Thalia would have speech therapy in a separate classroom only once per week for thirty minutes. Thalia was to have individual instruction and small group interactions during this time.

Donnie and Lorena were pleased with Thalia's first grade performance. They felt that the child study team's plan moving forward seemed appropriate. The move to Livingston solved a major problem for Donnie and Lorena. They were confident that Thalia was in a school district that was providing the support that they believed was required to satisfy her education and social behavior needs.

CHAPTER 23

EDUCATION AND SOCIAL BEHAVIOR PROGRESS IS NOT A STEADY, upward straight line. There are plateaus and, occasionally, setbacks. This reality is set in the challenge of schoolwork always being more demanding. The assignments are designed to be completed more independently with less teacher direction as a child gets older. Thalia's second grade teacher sensed early in the school year that some lessons could initially be difficult for Thalia and that it would take time for her to grasp some of the material that the class was learning. The teacher explained to Donnie and Lorena that the class would work on certain concepts throughout the year to calm their concerns.

A pattern emerged each year in elementary school of Thalia having to get familiar with her new teacher and classmates for her to perform her best. Thalia, even at this young age, needed to believe that a teacher thought that she could do well. Thalia also had to feel that a teacher was trying to help her succeed. Patience and understanding were required from Thalia's teachers. As was creating an environment where Thalia felt comfortable in the classroom and motivated to learn. Thalia was encouraged and her confidence was boosted in a supportive classroom atmosphere. Developing a friendly relationship with a teacher was often the difference.

Teachers were able to notice that Thalia put forth a dedicated effort toward her schoolwork. They did not question Thalia's desire to achieve. The second grade teacher reported that Thalia is, "a hard-working member of our class," and that, "she displays a positive attitude in class." Thalia was described as a lovely girl and a joy to have in class. The teachers found Thalia to have an outgoing personality. The second grade teacher commented to Donnie and Lorena that Thalia was, "well-liked by her peers." Thalia did not present any disciplinary problems. Thalia also stopped the habit of telling her classmates if they were doing something wrong.

Thalia was on grade level for reading and language arts, math, social studies, and science. Math remained the subject that presented the greatest difficulty. Thalia had the same struggles as in first grade of recalling basic facts and applying the appropriate problem-solving strategies. Thalia had trouble understanding the newly introduced math concepts. The concern about Thalia's math skills was evidenced in her performance on the Stanford Achievement Test, a standardized test that was administered for different grade levels. Thalia took the Stanford Achievement Test in March of her second grade year. Thalia scored in the below-average range in the sections that tested math problem-solving and math procedures. Thalia's teacher could report only a slight improvement in math throughout the year.

Thalia had overall strengths in spelling. She was developing a greater awareness of the words that she used in her written and verbal communication. Thalia was improving at structuring sentences, with errors only occasionally noted. She showed some ability for creative writing if she received assistance. Thalia improved at recalling what she was reading, retelling the story, and relating her experiences to the story. Prompting might be needed to help Thalia convey her thoughts. Thalia scored in the average range on the reading section of the Stanford Achievement Test in word study skills, reading vocabulary, reading comprehension, language, and spelling.

Thalia showed the most growth in her speech therapy sessions. This remained the environment where she was the most comfortable. Thalia's social skills were apparent in this setting. She initiated conversations frequently and she was able to maintain her attention throughout the interactions. What Thalia was saying during these conversations was almost always on topic. The progress was to the point where it was decided that speech therapy would not be needed when Thalia entered third grade.

Lorena agreed to Thalia no longer receiving speech therapy, but she expressed trepidation to the child study team about Thalia losing her individual classroom aide as well. Thalia responded well to one-on-one instruction. The aide was instrumental in making sure that Thalia understood assignment directions. The aide provided the guidance that Thalia needed to complete certain tasks. The child study team agreed to Lorena's request. It was felt by Thalia's teachers that the aide remained vital for her development in the larger classroom setting.

Much of Thalia's academic problems continued to stem from her having a short attention span and her losing focus. The second grade teacher identified Thalia's being easily distracted and her talking with other classmates as the main factors that impeded her learning. Thalia's focus could drift. It was not an issue on some days, but a major problem on others. How often the teacher and the aide had to refocus Thalia also varied by the subject area. Thalia's losing focus caused her to miss parts of lessons. The teacher and the aide would have to repeatedly redirect Thalia's attention to what was being said in class. Thalia's keeping up with the pace of the class was becoming a greater issue. Thalia would then feel overwhelmed and get upset when she could not quickly grasp a new concept or come up with the answers to questions.

Assignment directions were once again given in a short, simple, and straightforward manner to help Thalia maintain her focus. The directions continued to be repeated by the aide as needed. The third grade teacher and the aide came up with the idea of having Thalia repeat the directions back to them so that they knew if she understood an assignment.

New strategies were implemented to help Thalia organize her school materials and reduce any confusion. Organization checklists were created. The teacher's aide and Thalia would start the school day by taking everything out of her backpack. The teacher's aide first made sure that Thalia put her lunchbox in the classroom lunch basket so that it was one less item taking up space and distracting her. The teacher's aide and Thalia could more easily point out exactly what she needed for each subject that day with everything removed from her backpack and placed on the table. It was also set up that Thalia received a copy of class notes so that she did not have to worry about missing something that was said in class, although her note-taking was considered to be good.

Math continued to be the most troublesome subject for Thalia when she was in third grade. The teacher tried various strategies with Thalia to improve her math skills. This extra help did not produce the desired outcome. It was decided that Thalia would be pulled out of the general education classroom for forty minutes every day to have math class in the resource room.

Being pulled out of the general education classroom brought on a new and different conflict for Thalia. Thalia became more aware of having to sort through aspects related to her learning disability as she got older. Thalia did not like leaving the general education classroom for her specialized learning. Thalia felt that she was being singled out by having to go to a different classroom. The special education math teacher would come to the classroom door and get Thalia to go to the resource room. It was noticeable to the other children. The students all knew where Thalia was going. Thalia was embarrassed. She was nervous about what her classmates might think of her. Thalia told Lorena that it was, "not fair." Thalia asked her mother why she could not learn like everyone else. More disheartening was that Thalia referred to being pulled out of the general education classroom when talking to Lorena as her going to, "stupid class."

Lorena was crushed in hearing that her daughter thought of herself in that way. Lorena tried to discuss with Thalia why taking math in a different classroom was necessary. Lorena told Thalia that it was intended only to help her. Lorena assured Thalia that it was not a form of punishment and that she did not do anything wrong. Lorena explained to Thalia that she would appreciate the help that she was receiving when she got older.

Lorena could tell that the bothersome aspect of Thalia having math class in the resource room was her anxiety about the other students' perceptions. Lorena kept reminding Thalia that everyone learns differently. She stressed to Thalia that everyone is good at some things and needs help at others. Lorena told Thalia that having to take one subject in another classroom does not make her stupid, just different. Lorena also said to Thalia to not let anyone put her down. Lorena was not completely sure how much of this was registering with her eight-year-old daughter who simply wanted to be like the rest of her classmates. Lorena started to stick notes of love and encouragement in Thalia's lunchbox to help her deal with the situation.

Thalia's fear of how she was being perceived by her classmates created another problem that impacted her academic performance. Thalia became more concerned about what other students in the class were doing rather than concentrating on her work. Thalia, after being observed and evaluated all of these years, developed a sense that people were always looking at her. She felt pressure. Thalia wanted to be seen as keeping up with her peers. Thalia might find it intimidating to see other students completing their work quickly and seemingly without any difficulty, while she was struggling to finish assignments.

Thalia's response was to try to be one of the first students in the class to finish an assignment. Being the first student to complete an assignment was in her mind an accomplishment. Finishing quickly for Thalia meant success in that she would be thought of as smart by her classmates. Thalia was careless and she did not always check her answers when she worked in this manner. Rushing through an assignment led to Thalia not performing at a level that she was capable of had she taken her time.

Writing was the one skill where the combination of Thalia's having trouble focusing and her working quickly produced an inconsistent performance. Thalia loved to read and it was often her choice for an independent activity. Thalia's teachers found her to be developing nicely in reading fluency. She was always reading on grade level. Her reading ability could be thought to translate to having the skill of using words effectively. Writing, however, requires critical thought and elaboration on the words that are chosen and how the sentences and paragraphs are constructed and organized.

Thalia had a hard time getting started on writing projects. She did not know where to begin when trying to write. She struggled with brainstorming and choosing a topic to write about. She needed a great amount of guidance in generating ideas and putting those ideas into words. Thalia had difficulty establishing a clear purpose or main idea in her writing once a topic was chosen. Thalia was not able to sufficiently use descriptive language or offer the necessary details to support her ideas. The teacher tried having Thalia verbalize her thoughts before writing them. This strategy had varying degrees of success. Thalia's teacher in third grade felt that her writing skills were regressing.

Thalia had another conflict when completing writing assignments. She was reluctant to make any changes suggested by her teacher or her aide to what she wrote. Thalia thought that editing and revising her writing was extra work that she was being given. Thalia felt that she was being punished for not writing well on the first try. It was clear that writing was a task that did not produce confidence, but rather frequent irritation.

Thalia's frustration led to a brief period where she would challenge her teachers. She did not always want to follow directions. Thalia, at times, used a disrespectful tone with her teacher. She reverted to being defensive. Thalia would get rigid and she could even become argumentative. Her third grade teacher wrote in December of the school year that, "it is a pleasure to work with Thalia this year. She is a sweet and well-mannered child who is eager." That teacher soon after indicated to Donnie and Lorena that Thalia needed to be a better classroom citizen.

This was the first time that Thalia was asked to improve her classroom demeanor since the rare instances of non-compliance at the DLC, when she was four years old. The teacher wanted Thalia to display better self-control, be more courteous, and take responsibility for her actions. Thalia interpreted some of the contentious exchanges that the teachers did not like her. Thalia would say to Lorena that the teachers were mean and that they did not want to help her.

Lorena could pick up on this frustration by seeing how Thalia acted at home. Lorena was noticing that the issues that resulted from Thalia's disability overtook her at times. Lorena always tried to talk to Thalia about what happened at school. Thalia would become quiet. She had feelings of helplessness. Thalia felt alone. Thalia would question why God made her this way. Lorena told Thalia that it was because of the big plans that God had for her.

Lorena, incorrectly, blamed herself for whatever challenges Thalia was going through. It was hard for Lorena to see Thalia coming home from school crying because she did not understand a lesson or an assignment. Lorena's strategy was to tell Thalia to calm down, go to her room, and write down her thoughts. When Thalia felt better, she and Lorena would talk about the situation. Lorena assured Thalia that they were going to figure out the problem, and that it was alright if it took some time to get to the right answer.

With Lorena's constant encouragement, Thalia's acting out in frustration in school was not a long-term behavior. The same teacher who expressed some displeasure with Thalia's classroom attitude remarked at the end of the year that she enjoyed working with Thalia and that she was proud of her growth. Thalia's third grade teacher described that she put forth a greater effort in the final three months of the school year. The teacher added that Thalia was using a more respectful tone. As her teachers pointed out some behavior issues earlier in the school year, they all indicated that there was substantial improvement when Thalia became more comfortable in her environment.

Thalia's inability to always focus during lessons did persist until the end of the third grade school year. Some of the problems of this nature were not going to be resolved overnight or with a couple of discussions between a teacher and Thalia. These were deep-rooted behaviors that existed because of a learning disability that would take time for Thalia to figure out how to manage at various stages of her life.

CHAPTER 24

THE LATEST STRATEGY THAT WAS USED WITH THALIA IN trying to help her focus and alleviate her frustration was encouraging her to participate in class discussions. Thalia raised her hand to respond to a teacher's question only when she was certain that she knew the answer. Thalia felt that giving a wrong answer might result in her classmates mocking her. Thalia found it unsettling when a classmate put forth an idea or an answer to a question during a class discussion that she did not know.

Thalia's third grade science teacher, in particular, believed that an increase in participation during class would help her understand the concepts that she was learning, help maintain her focus, and overcome her getting distracted. The science teacher figured out that Thalia responded well to personal attention and positive reinforcement through verbal praise. Extending that type of encouragement to Thalia was the first step to getting her to be more engaged in class.

Thalia responded well to the teacher's praise. The science teacher was able to get Thalia to more frequently participate in class discussions by the end of the school year. The science teacher was proven correct in how Thalia's participation positively influenced her academic performance. Thalia became excited about the lessons and the science experiments conducted in class. She showed a better ability to retain information. Thalia was comfortable asking questions of the science teacher for clarification if she did not understand concepts and assignments. Thalia eagerly and thoroughly finished her work once she understood what was being asked of her. She was easily completing writing assignments in science class. Thalia never had any trouble finding a group or working well with the other students during a group exercise, which was often used as the learning method in science class. The science teacher found Thalia to be a content student who displayed a good attitude in class.

Thalia still did not like the obvious act of leaving the general education classroom. The shifting of having math in the resource room, however, created a comfort level for Thalia that started to produce the desired results in that subject. Thalia was better able to maintain her focus in math. She responded well to the small group interaction in this learning environment. Thalia was recalling the basic math facts and used what she learned to solve a variety of math problems.

Thalia had to overcome being impulsive when learning math. Thalia would get stuck on an inconsequential point rather than the key aspect that would lead to her solving the problem. The math teacher commented, "once her behavior is brought to her attention, she tries very diligently to attend to the lesson. Once she understands the lesson, she works independently with her group and is able to follow directions." There was an improvement in all aspects of math class by the end of the year. It was decided at the end of the year IEP meeting that Thalia was to continue being pulled out of the general education classroom to have math in the resource room for fourth grade. This meant that she would have the same math teacher.

Thalia ended third grade with her numerous strengths identified in the final year IEP as, "eye contact, communicating needs, completing work, interaction with peers." It was noted that Thalia displayed an "understanding of respect for her peers and teachers." Thalia was described in the IEP as, "a very sweet child with a positive attitude, which helps her learning to no end." It was also highlighted that Thalia benefited from, "the support she receives from her family."

There was the decision at the final IEP meeting that Thalia would have a shared teacher's aide for fourth grade. While this was another adjustment for Thalia, it was an indication of progress. Thalia also made it through her first school year of not having speech therapy without there being any thought of putting that back into her education plan.

Donnie and Lorena had to sift through an enormous amount of information that they were being told about their daughter's academic skills. There were report cards, IEP meetings, and conferences with all of her teachers. One final requirement in third grade was that Thalia had to take the New Jersey Assessment of Skills and Knowledge standardized test, NJ ASK. Thalia was able to take the test in a separate room with a small group of students. She was allowed additional time with frequent breaks provided. The directions were read aloud and repeated, clarified, or rephrased as needed. The test administrator had to ensure that Thalia answered all of the questions in a section.

The language arts section of NJ ASK had students complete

one writing task about a picture and one writing task about a poem. The test included a reading section where students had to answer questions that assessed their understanding of the information presented in a story. The math section tested students on a variety of problem-solving skills. Thalia was proficient in both language arts and math. She scored above the statewide student average for her grade in both subjects.

The fourth grade version of NJ ASK added a science section to the test. Thalia scored advanced proficient in science. Her language arts results remained at the proficient level. Thalia achieved a level of advanced proficiency in the math section of the NJ ASK test. This was one point of evidence that her taking math in the resource room with the same teacher was helping her improve in that subject.

Thalia's math teacher commented early in the school year in fourth grade, "Thalia has made strides in math due to her efforts and perseverance in class. If Thalia does not understand a skill, she asks suitable questions and applies the responses appropriately to her classwork. She is extremely conscientious about completing her homework and returning it on time. I am very proud of Thalia's efforts and dedication." In March, the math teacher continued with a complimentary assessment, writing that, "Thalia continues to work diligently in class. Her wonderful inquisitive attitude enables her to prosper with all of her skills." Now receiving letter grades in each subject, Thalia earned an A in math in all marking periods of the school year.

Thalia's general education classroom teacher in fourth grade found her to be a student who gave a great effort. The teacher described Thalia as, "a responsible, cooperative, and motivated student who has made steady progress in fourth grade. She takes her classwork very seriously and always tries to do her personal best in class. Thalia demonstrates a strong desire to learn by always asking questions and for clarifications of words and phrases."

The fourth grade teacher quickly picked up on the learning challenges that led to Thalia becoming frustrated when completing certain assignments. Thalia could again be stubborn in refusing suggestions. Thalia's teacher noticed that she would get defensive and was not always open to ideas and methods that could help her understand the material. The teacher remarked, "Thalia's strong will makes it challenging for her to accept teacher guidance and support."

Similar to the previous school year, the teacher figured out that Thalia worked effectively in one-on-one and small-group environments. The teacher learned that rephrasing directions was necessary. Thalia was encouraged to ask questions to clarify concepts and assignment directions. The teacher provided suggestions to better organize Thalia's classroom habits with structure and routine. The teacher also started to make a concerted effort to offer Thalia positive reinforcement through verbal praise.

These strategies were helpful as Thalia's teacher indicated by the end of the fourth grade school year that, "it has been a pleasure to watch Thalia grow this year. She has consistently demonstrated that she is a hardworking and responsible student and has made fine progress in fourth grade. She has shown growth in responding to suggestions and more readily accepts support when faced with academic challenges. Thalia should be commended for her desire to do her personal best work. Asking questions for clarification has been a successful tool for Thalia. It has been a pleasure to be her teacher." The teacher described that socially, Thalia seemed happy in class. The teacher reported that Thalia was a kind and caring member of the classroom who was making friends.

Thalia's support services were to remain the same for the fifth grade. She was to receive a shared teacher's aide. She was to continue being pulled out of her general education classroom for math in the resource room. It was going to be the third consecutive year that Thalia had math in this manner.

While Livingston was fulfilling all of Thalia's educational needs, it was a town that offered many community activities for children to become involved. Thalia was always willing to participate in activities outside of school. Donnie and Lorena enrolled Thalia in swimming and gymnastics class when she was young. Whereas swimming and gymnastics were more individual, Donnie and Lorena sought to get Thalia involved in activities that would have her socialize with other girls as part of a team or group. Donnie and Lorena knew the importance of having their daughter be around other girls her age in various settings. Participating in community activities allowed Thalia to meet children from town who were not in her elementary school, but who would later join her in middle school and high school. Donnie and Lorena hoped that these experiences and making friends with more girls would translate into Thalia being a bit more confident and less worried about how she was perceived at school.

Thalia played soccer and softball. Participating in sports could be challenging for a child. A singular child is the focus of everyone watching at times during a game, such as being at bat in a softball game. It is easy for a child to be ridiculed by other kids during moments of failure. Donnie was an assistant coach for Thalia's soccer and softball teams. It was a great way for him to spend time with his daughter. He was also able to keep an eye on her as she attempted these sports and adjusted to a different social environment.

Donnie bought a bat and ball for Thalia when she was four years old. Donnie took Thalia into the backyard and he taught her how to hold the bat and hit the ball. Thalia became upset when she was unable to hit the ball. Donnie explained to her that they would practice and keep trying. Donnie taught Thalia how to catch a softball much in the same way that she might have learned a skill in school, with a progression that made her comfortable. Donnie and Thalia initially played catch using a sponge ball. They then used a whiffle ball, before gradually getting to a softball that was used in games.

Thalia often played second base in her softball games. It was a shorter throw to first base, giving her more time to field the ball and complete the play. Donnie was elated the first time that Thalia fielded a ground ball and she made the throw to first base to get the runner out. Donnie and Lorena were proud of Thalia's willingness to participate in team sports. They knew that this was important in helping develop her social skills.

Thalia participated in the Girl Scouts throughout most of elementary school. It was another opportunity for Thalia to interact with girls her age outside of school. Thalia made new friends with some of the girls in her troop. Some of her friends' mothers served as the scout leaders, making Thalia comfortable in this setting. Thalia liked the activities that she participated in with the Girls Scouts. She sold cookies to raise money for her troop, with her many family members among her best customers. The Girl Scouts also went on a variety of educational trips that Thalia enjoyed.

Thalia participated in dance class for five years. Thalia learned various styles of dance, starting with jazz and tap. Thalia learned routines in Broadway-style dance and hip-hop as she got older. Thalia performed routines at her recitals in groups with other girls. Rehearsing her dance routines was preferable to practicing sports. Participating in dance gave Thalia a better indication as to what she could accomplish at a non-academic activity when she put in the time and effort.

CHAPTER 25

THALIA HAD BEEN EVALUATED, OBSERVED, AND QUESTIONED about her learning capabilities and social behavior since she was two-and-a-half years old. In July 2007, one month before her tenth birthday and two months before starting fifth grade, Thalia had an appointment with the second pediatric neurologist who examined her when she was initially evaluated for autism. It was the first time in over five years that this particular doctor examined Thalia.

The doctor quickly detected that Thalia did not have any of the prominent autism spectrum behavior features that she showed as a younger child. Thalia did not display any repetitive language or self-stimulating behaviors. Thalia's eye contact with the doctor was good during the examination. She looked away from the doctor only briefly at times. Thalia's speech was clear, although a bit soft-spoken as she talked to the doctor. It was easy for the doctor to see that Thalia's communication skills greatly improved.

The doctor asked Thalia some math questions. Thalia correctly multiplied four times three after a brief pause. Thalia was not able to compute six times seven. The doctor felt that any academic weaknesses could be addressed by providing the appropriate teaching resources. The doctor was more concerned with her overall behavior characteristics than with her math skills.

Thalia was comfortable and acted appropriately throughout the visit. She was smiling as she talked with the doctor. Thalia asked the doctor sensible questions. Thalia even told the doctor a joke. She quizzed the doctor, "what goes ninety-nine, clunk?" When the doctor said that he did not know the answer, Thalia told him, "a centipede with a wooden leg." The doctor chuckled. Thalia was then asked to explain the joke to the doctor, which she did.

The doctor responded by telling Thalia a joke. The doctor asked Thalia, "why did the penny jump off the cliff and not the quarter?" The doctor answered his riddle when Thalia did not immediately respond, telling her, "because the quarter had more cents (sense)." Thalia laughed and, more importantly, she correctly explained the double meaning of the riddle.

Thalia still had the diagnosis of Pervasive Development Disorder/Autism that placed her on the autism spectrum for all of her school district records. The doctor concluded after this examination that Thalia was neurologically intact and that she was without any observable signs of the disability. Thalia's new official diagnosis was Post Pervasive Development Disorder with Autistic Features. It would be the last time that Thalia was examined by a pediatric neurologist.

Donnie and Lorena were thrilled with this diagnosis. It provided a clear indication of Thalia's substantial improvement. They viewed it as a triumph for all of the tremendous sacrifice and effort that Thalia put in throughout the years. Donnie and Lorena did have some apprehension that the newly diagnosed status might convey to people, particularly the Livingston child study team, that Thalia was cured and that her behavior problems were completely solved. Donnie and Lorena were concerned that Thalia would lose all of her special education support services.

A comprehensive review of special education students is conducted every three years as required by New Jersey state law. The purpose of this review is to update a student's disability classification, offer additional guidance for the end-of-school-year IEP meeting, and assist in developing the following school year's education plan. Thalia's pediatric neurologist evaluation in July was one part of this information gathering process.

Thalia's remaining evaluations occurred in March and April of her fifth grade year. The timing of the required comprehensive review was crucial as Thalia was finishing her last year in elementary school and she would be attending a different school for sixth grade. The required triennial review consisted of a psychological evaluation and an educational evaluation. A psychiatric evaluation of Thalia was later requested by the Livingston child study team as well.

Thalia was evaluated by the school psychologist on March 7 and 8. Thalia readily accompanied the psychologist to the testing room for the assessment. The psychologist found Thalia's attitude toward the testing process to be friendly and cooperative. Thalia, however, did ask many questions. Thalia wanted to know why she was being tested. She asked the psychologist, "will the teachers get blamed if I do something wrong?" The psychologist assured Thalia that they would not.

Thalia made consistent eye contact with the psychologist throughout the assessment. There was an easily established and maintained rapport. The psychologist felt that Thalia was motivated to do well in this examination. Thalia's comfortable disposition during the test allowed the psychologist to conclude that the evaluation should be regarded as a good estimate of her current level of intellectual functioning.

The psychologist put Thalia through a range of tests. Thalia was presented with two words that represented common objects or concepts. She had to describe how they were similar. Thalia had to give definitions of words that the psychologist read to her. Visual tests were conducted. Thalia was presented with two or three rows of pictures. She had to choose one picture from each row to form a group with a common characteristic.

The psychologist tested Thalia's attention and concentration. Thalia performed well when she had to read a sequence of numbers and letters and then had to recall the numbers in ascending order and the letters in alphabetical order. Thalia had trouble when she had to read a sequence of numbers and then had to repeat the numbers in the order that they were given, and in the reverse order.

Thalia's overall results on the psychological testing placed her in the average range when compared to other children her age. This outcome indicated that Thalia would be expected to acquire academic material at a similar rate to her same-aged peers. The psychological testing revealed that Thalia was stronger in visual learning than verbal instruction.

The education assessment occurred in April. The separate interviews that were conducted with Thalia's general education classroom teacher and her math teacher were critical components of the education assessment. Thalia's math teacher, who was now in the third year of working with her, reported that Thalia improved her recall of concepts and that she was applying them correctly in problem-solving. The math problems that required several steps to solve continued to cause the most difficulty. The teacher pointed out that Thalia was relaxed and attentive during math class in the resource room. Thalia was repeatedly asking questions to clarify new material. Thalia remained extremely reliable in turning in her homework, something that all of her teachers could see as an indication of her effort. The math teacher made a point in the interview to express that the improvement in Thalia's skills was due to all of her hard work.

The general education classroom teacher mentioned that Thalia showed improvement in her ability to follow assignment directions. Thalia was getting better at staying on task for an extended period of time and seeing it to completion. Thalia's maintaining her focus persisted as a concern on the tougher assignments. The teacher noted Thalia's tendency to become frustrated. Thalia's teachers were communicating similar sentiments directly to Donnie and Lorena. The comments that came from this evaluation were not a surprise.

The teacher emphasized in the interview that writing was Thalia's most challenging academic task. Thalia remained anxious when she had to complete a writing assignment. The teacher explained that Thalia had trouble generating ideas and providing supportive detail on what she was writing about. The teacher stated that a variety of techniques were being discussed in class. It was noted that Thalia participated in a Writer's Workshop at school that exposed her to additional strategies as well.

Thalia's teacher would guide her in many writing exercises to practice these new strategies as a way to boost her confidence. Thalia was still having difficulty incorporating all of these strategies into her writing when she worked independently. Thalia also continued to be reluctant to make the suggested changes from the teacher or her aide that would enhance her writing. The teacher did remark that Thalia was always prepared for her writing lessons and that she was putting forth a good effort to improve that skill.

The general education teacher mentioned Thalia's continued habit of working quickly, which when writing caused her not to elaborate on ideas and to not be thorough in checking her work. The teacher provided examples where Thalia's writing hastily led to her inconsistent and, at times, careless performance.

Working quickly was especially impeding Thalia's performance on in-class assignments. Thalia had to perform at that moment when doing an in-class assignment or taking a test. Thalia had more time to figure out what needed to be done when doing homework assignments. Completing assignments at home also meant that no other students were there to see how long it took her to finish a task. Thalia was again consumed with being the first student to finish an in-class assignment, which everyone could notice.

The general education teacher highlighted that Thalia enjoyed reading. Thalia's love of reading was on full display in the "Battle of the Books" competition earlier in the school year. Students were required to read three books. Thalia read six. The teacher wrote to Donnie and Lorena that Thalia's performance on this reading challenge demonstrated, "initiative, self-discipline, and a proactive approach to her development as a reader and a learner." The teacher assessed that Thalia's reading comprehension was on grade level. The teacher felt that Thalia's critical thinking skills about what she read still needed to be developed. Critical thinking was another characteristic hindering her writing skills and the elaboration of her ideas.

The problem when students struggle with writing is that it influences their performance in the completion of assignments in many of their subjects. Thalia was encouraged by many of her teachers to provide more detail in her written assignments. One way that the teachers believed that her writing could be improved was if she was more confident in her command of the subject material.

Similar to previous years in school, some teachers wanted Thalia to participate more in class as a way to advance her understanding of a subject's concepts. Thalia's social studies teacher expressed a desire that Thalia have, "more consistent participation so she can take ownership of her learning." Thalia's science teacher found that Thalia was always attentive in class discussions and had a good understanding of the concepts, but wished that she participated more.

Thalia was observed in the general education classroom during an integrated reading and language arts lesson as part of the education evaluation. Thalia responded appropriately when the class was asked by the teacher to take out the materials that were needed for the lesson. Thalia and her classmates were given multi-step directions about how to create, label, and order a set of folders that would assist them in organizing the information that was needed to complete a personal essay assignment. Thalia often repeated directions to the teacher or her aide before starting an assignment of this complexity to ensure that she was doing it correctly. Thalia did the same for this assignment.

Thalia succeeded in following all of the directions. She then realized that the teacher accidentally gave an incorrect direction on the assignment regarding the order in which the folders were to be organized. Thalia was the only student in the class to pick up on the mistake. Thalia pointed out the error to the teacher. The teacher recognized Thalia's observation and announced the correct information to the class.

The teacher gave instructions to the students about how they were to write the first paragraph of their personal essays. Thalia needed assistance on this part of the assignment. Thalia was having difficulty putting her thoughts into written words. Thalia received support and encouragement from her teacher and the aide to eventually produce the paragraph.

The education evaluation continued with a series of tests on April 8. Thalia was told by her teacher's aide that she was going to be meeting with a member of the child study team and that she would be tested later that afternoon. Thalia was uneasy upon hearing this sudden news. She told her aide, "I didn't know that I had a test today. I didn't have a study guide for the test. I don't want to take it. Why am I the only one who has to do this?"

The child study team examiner arrived to administer the test and explained to Thalia what she was going to be required to do. The examiner assured Thalia that studying for this type of test was not needed. Thalia understood and she willingly went to the testing room. Thalia did continue to ask several questions as to the purpose of the test. The child study team examiner's responses were able to satisfy Thalia.

The examiner asked Thalia about her interests in school. Thalia responded that she didn't like math that much, but that, "the problem-solving part is not so bad." Thalia said that she liked science and social studies. She told the examiner that she liked reading and language arts, "a little bit." Thalia mentioned that she was reading a book in a series titled, *Baby Mouse*. Thalia then said that writing is, "so-so," and that she liked, "grammar stuff like predicates, but not journal writing."

Thalia responded, "this is too hard," or, "I didn't learn that yet," if the questions or tasks posed by the child study team examiner presented difficulty. Thalia showed adequate focus during the test, but she fidgeted with her pencil as an indication of some discomfort. Thalia was asked to read aloud a long passage that was on a fifth grade reading level. Thalia read with well-developed expression, fluency, intonation, and phrasing. Thalia, however, read at a rapid rate which affected her ability to comprehend what she was reading. Thalia correctly answered some questions about the vocabulary and story details in the passage. Thalia had greater difficulty when she had to respond to the questions about the main theme of the story and its sequencing. Thalia's answers to these types of questions were limited in detail. She had trouble explaining her main points.

The examiner asked Thalia to read aloud a passage that was considered on a fourth grade reading level. The child study team member conducting the evaluation instructed Thalia to read at a slower rate. Thalia demonstrated her ability to comprehend what she was reading at a much higher level when reading slower and reading this slightly easier passage. Thalia was better able to answer questions about the main theme, details, and sequencing of the story. Thalia still needed prompting to clarify her answers and to explain her points quickly and more concisely.

Thalia's listening skills were tested by the examiner reading a short passage to her and her having to supply a missing word. Thalia had to listen to a sequence of audio-recorded instructions and follow the directions of pointing to various objects in a picture. The number of details of the audio-recorded stories increased throughout this section of the test.

Thalia's writing skills were assessed by her being asked to formulate and write sentences quickly. Thalia was presented with a picture and a set of three words that had to be included in the sentence. Thalia often struggled with classroom writing assignments, but her spelling, sentence structure, and quality of written expression on this exercise were excellent. This result did not seem typical of when Thalia had to do writing assignments in class. Thalia's performance showed that when she had enough information given to her, especially visually, she could put it together in a logical manner. The writing assignments where Thalia had to brainstorm a topic, creatively put her ideas into words, and support her main points with sufficient details were the tasks that presented difficulty.

Thalia was able to solve problems involving addition, subtraction, multiplication, money, and time on the math tests that were part of the education evaluation. She had some difficulty solving problems of division, fractions, and measurement.

The child study team decided at a meeting in April that it needed additional information to determine Thalia's eligibility for special education services and to better develop her IEP for the following school year. There were worries about Thalia's communication skills and her social or emotional behavior, especially her anxious and frustration tendencies. An evaluation by a psychiatrist was requested. Lorena, again, was quick to have thoughts of blaming herself for Thalia having to deal with any anxious traits that precipitated the need for this type of examination.

Thalia met with a psychiatrist on April 16. Lorena explained to the psychiatrist that the purpose of the appointment was because the Livingston child study team members, "just want to evaluate her." Lorena indicated early in the visit that Thalia was going to enter middle school the following year. Lorena emphasized that she was concerned that Thalia might no longer receive the support services that had been essential to her education and behavior development.

Lorena provided the psychiatrist with background information about Thalia. She described her daughter as, "sweet, caring, and sensitive to others' pain." Lorena noted that Thalia tended to excessively worry about things daily. Thalia would worry about a test and school assignments. Thalia thrived with structure. She liked to be completely organized. Lorena explained that Thalia became anxious any time she felt unprepared or her thoughts were not in order. Even on a family trip, Thalia wanted to make sure that she was prepared for what the weather might be and organized with what clothes she was going to wear on a particular day. Thalia wanted to constantly know the activities that they were going to be doing while on vacation. Thalia liked having a planned schedule.

Lorena informed the psychiatrist that Thalia did not have any history of mental health treatment. Lorena added that Thalia did not experience anxiety attacks, nor did she engage in any obsessive-compulsive behaviors. Lorena did state that Thalia could become overwhelmed and get agitated when things did not go her way. She exhibited brief outbursts of frustration when she was having to learn a new concept or confront a new idea. Thalia could get stuck on a certain thought and have difficulty letting it go as the only way to approach a problem. It was these preoccupations and her rigidness that led to the occasional antagonistic moments between Thalia and her teachers.

Thalia was a bit panicked in the waiting room as the psychiatrist spoke with Lorena. Thalia was highly interested in what her mother and the doctor were discussing. She interrupted their conversation multiple times. Thalia expressed concern about the outcome of this evaluation. She was old enough to understand that her performance on all of these assessments influenced how she would experience school. Thalia mentioned to the psychiatrist during their session that she was nervous about her possible classroom placement.

The psychiatrist found Thalia to be cooperative during the examination. Thalia's speech was purposive and goal-directed. Thalia was responsive to the psychiatrist's questions. Thalia delivered her answers at a rate that indicated that she was relaxed during the session. The psychiatrist felt that Thalia's insights and judgments were appropriate. Thalia was alert throughout the session, although her eye contact varied slightly when she spoke.

The psychiatrist asked Thalia a series of questions to learn her thoughts on a variety of topics. Thalia described her family as, "very nice to me. Sometimes they give me a little agita." She described her school experience as, "I'm not struggling in school, but I still don't really like it. Most kids don't like school." Thalia said to the psychiatrist about her demeanor, "my emotions are usually the same." Thalia was asked to identify her three wishes. She responded, "number one, a cell phone, number two, a laptop, number three, power to fly." She commented in response to another question that if she could be a non-human creature she would be, "a chipmunk. They are cute."

Overall, the psychiatrist felt that it was important in any plan moving forward to recognize that Thalia had strengths in cognitive ability and that she possessed academic potential. The psychiatrist noted that Thalia had several areas of interest. The psychiatrist also pointed out that Thalia had a very supportive family. The psychiatrist's diagnostic impression was that Thalia had Generalized Anxiety Disorder. The anxiety would cause Thalia's propensity for feeling on edge and becoming preoccupied with worries or other negative thoughts.

The psychiatrist believed that there was nothing to indicate that Thalia met the criteria for Pervasive Developmental Disorder/ Autism. The psychiatrist, however, felt that there were residuals of Thalia having that disorder. The psychiatrist highlighted that Thalia's disability could create conditions of misreading social cues, inflexibility, rigidity, and low frustration tolerance. The psychiatrist reported that all of these characteristics, "may result in angry episodes which do appear to impact upon her level of functioning in the school-based setting."

The psychiatrist offered a series of recommendations to assist Thalia. The first recommendation was about Thalia's learning environment. The psychiatrist claimed that Thalia would benefit from the appropriate structure, support, and supervision with the use of positive reinforcement. The psychiatrist did not provide any specifics as to what satisfying these environmental conditions would entail. The psychiatrist instead encouraged that there be close coordination between the child study team and the family in making those determinations.

The psychiatrist suggested that Thalia might benefit from regularly seeing a behavior psychologist. A behavior psychologist could assist Thalia in identifying the items that caused her the greatest anxiety. This type of therapy might help Thalia recognize the early warning signs of her anxiety. Thalia could also be introduced to relaxation and keeping calm techniques. There was a suggestion that a social skills component to psychological behavior therapy could benefit Thalia. This social skills therapy would include group role play, receiving feedback to enhance interactions, and social problem-solving.

The psychiatrist mentioned that treatment through medication could be considered if the behavior and social skills strategies were not effective. The symptoms to be most aware of were if Thalia's excessive worry and rigid thinking continued to where it was evident in multiple settings and to the point where it impacted her level of functioning.

Lorena conveyed a willingness to consider a behavior psychologist with social skills therapy. Lorena instantly sensed that Thalia was insulted and upset by this suggestion. Thalia had some informal conversations with a school counselor, but she ended up never being treated by a behavior psychologist. Lorena was less enthused about the option of medication. Thalia would not at any time be prescribed medication for her autism spectrum disability or her Generalized Anxiety Disorder.

Lorena was encouraged by the psychiatrist to use some basic stress-reducing techniques with Thalia. Lorena discussed with Thalia counting to ten before saying anything that she might regret. They practiced talking calmly. Lorena made a greater effort to have mother/daughter time, such as going out to breakfast or doing an activity that Thalia enjoyed. Donnie and Lorena also constantly reinforced to Thalia that they will always love her and that nothing could happen that would change their support for her.

The IEP for sixth grade was created through her teachers' evaluations and the information gathered in the comprehensive triennial review. It was determined that Thalia continued to meet the criteria of eligibility for special education support services based on the category of her showing signs of being emotionally disturbed. The emotionally disturbed condition was described as potentially impacting Thalia's social functioning. The concerns were that Thalia could get impulsive, easily distracted, and overwhelmed with anxiety to such an extent that it impeded her learning and academic achievement.

Donnie and Lorena absolutely hated the emotionally disturbed disability classification. It was extremely bothersome as being emotionally disturbed from their perspective conjured up a person who did not have family support or any friends, or might be violent. Thalia had none of those situations, nor did she possess any of those personality characteristics. Donnie and Lorena were forced to accept this classification because it allowed Thalia to continue to receive the education support services that they believed their daughter still needed.

Some justification for the emotionally disturbed classification from the child study team's perspective was because several teachers and evaluators cited that Thalia's anxiety led to her displaying irrational fears. One teacher elaborated in the IEP report, stating that Thalia, "works hard to stay organized and to understand instructions given to her. She can get overwhelmed and anxious." Again, as Thalia's comfort level in the environment improved, so did her academic and social performance. The same teacher remarked, "since September, I have noted that she is better able to talk with a teacher in the room for clarity on an assignment and the anxiety usually lowers. She is persistent on tasks when she is able to focus herself, which on some days seems to be difficult for her to accomplish." The teacher found that Thalia, "looks forward to teacher praise and acceptance."

The teacher added at the end of the year that Thalia, "had a good year both academically and socially. She has become proficient in many skills and concepts in all content areas and worked especially hard to improve her writing skills. She has been a pleasure to have in class." The teacher encouraged Thalia to engage in journal writing over the summer to continue practicing that skill. Thalia participated in a summer book club as reading remained one of her most enjoyable activities.

The plan for sixth grade at her new school was for Thalia to continue to be placed in a general education classroom. She would have a shared teacher's aide. Thalia would receive additional in-class support for reading and language arts. Thalia was to experience orientation activities for transitioning to middle school along with her classmates.

CHAPTER 26

Livingston's Mount Pleasant Middle School was where the district's sixth grade students attended. The middle school was connected to one of the town's elementary school buildings. Thalia would then, along with her classmates, attend Livingston's Heritage Middle School for seventh and eighth grade. Livingston's middle school setup was such that the students attended three different schools in three years. It was the second time in Thalia's schooling that she had to make this consecutive-year adjustment.

The transition to middle school meant that the comforts of elementary school that Thalia enjoyed were all gone. There was no more familiarity with the building, knowing all of her classmates, and having the same math teacher in the resource room. Middle school involved more students, navigating a larger building, and the responsibility of walking independently from class to class. Being organized was harder in that Thalia had a locker instead of a desk. Thalia had to figure out which books and class materials to have with her at which point in the school day. Thalia had to adjust to more teachers in middle school than she interacted with in elementary school. Each subject teacher had to learn Thalia's strengths and weaknesses, as well as how to get her comfortable and motivated so that she could perform her best. The learning material and assignments were continuing to be more difficult.

This list of unknowns upon entering middle school could cause anxiety for any child. These concerns were magnified for someone who could be sensitive and prone to excessive worry. Thalia's ability to handle difficult situations was going to be tested in middle school. Donnie and Lorena were naturally apprehensive about Thalia attending a new school. They were preparing themselves if Thalia was going to have a hard time adjusting. They would have to interact with a different child study team and case manager for sixth grade and then for seventh and eighth grade as well.

Thalia adjusted relatively well to the middle school environment. She easily made her way around the building. Having a locker did not present any issues with her being organized throughout the school day. Thalia had some of her academic-related anxiety traits to sort through. Thalia continued to display nervousness about her grades. She desperately wanted to do well in school. Thalia was again becoming upset when she was not able to immediately figure out the concepts that a teacher was explaining or what she needed to do to complete an assignment. Thalia might be quick to say when the lessons became more complex that she, was, "not good at that subject."

Thalia's middle school teachers could sense her feeling uneasy when she was having difficulty in class. They could especially notice her getting increasingly tense when she was taking a test and she had trouble coming up with some of the answers. The stress alone might cause Thalia to miss a question that she would have otherwise known the answer. Thalia had to push herself through those feelings. The teachers would encourage Thalia during tests. The teachers knew that Thalia would achieve better results if she could just relax. The teachers could see that Thalia was a conscientious student through her worrisome tendencies. They all thought that Thalia desired to understand what she was learning and perform well in what she was being asked to do.

Thalia's anxiousness was compounded by her tendency to want to complete her assignments without any assistance. Thalia's independent characteristic can be illustrated as far back as her time at the DLC and her not wanting one of the teachers to help her draw a picture. Years later, Thalia was still determined to finish her schoolwork almost completely on her own. She might accept minimal prompting in the direction of the answer, but Thalia did not respond well to constantly receiving suggestions or being implored to revise her work in a certain way. Thalia perceived accepting assistance as a defeat. It served as an admission that she was not capable of doing what was required. Lorena would review some of Thalia's assignments with her, but even she was permitted to help only so much.

Preferring to work in this independent manner was problematic in the areas where Thalia did need assistance. This was apparent in one area of her reading. Thalia read fluently and she always remained on grade level. Thalia was having difficulty applying meaning to what she read. Thalia's teachers wanted her to analyze the material in such a way that it provided larger life lessons and enhanced her situational awareness. Thalia might get stuck on an incorrect thought. What Thalia was reading had greater significance when she was open to suggestions about how to evaluate a story's theme and its characteristics. Thalia would be given guiding questions by the teacher as a way to help her interpret what she was reading.

Math remained a challenging subject. Thalia had to constantly deal with the anxiety that came with not being able to quickly figure out the newly introduced concepts. One major adjustment to sixth grade for Thalia was how her math class was delivered. All of the students entering sixth grade had to take a placement test to determine the math class that they would be enrolled. The school divided the math classes into three tiers based on a student's skill level: advanced, average-performing, and underperforming. Thalia was placed in the underperforming skill level tier. The school then divided the students into teams. Thalia was assigned to a team that had one section of math for the underperforming students.

One math teacher was assigned to each team. The teacher for Thalia's math class consistently gave her the impression of not wanting to teach the underperforming skill level section. Thalia needed the teacher to be patient with her. Thalia perceived the teacher as being agitated when she had a hard time grasping the math concepts. Thalia did not feel that the teacher was rooting for her to succeed. It was the opposite of the nurturing environment Thalia had in math class from third through fifth grade.

Thalia dreaded going to math class for all of the sixth grade. It was a combination of learning material that she found difficult and an unsettling atmosphere. Thalia's math teacher encouraged her to take the initiative to ask for extra help. Thalia never felt comfortable enough to do so. Math remained a struggle throughout the school year. As it turned out, the school stopped using the tier system to create its math classes for the following year.

Aside from the discomfort in math class, many of the teachers in sixth grade figured out that visual prompts, repeating directions, and positive feedback were effective learning techniques for Thalia.

Teachers continued to encourage Thalia to participate in class as a way to reduce her anxiety and improve her performance. Thalia's habit of responding to a question in class only when she was completely confident of the answer remained. Thalia did thrive when working on small group projects, especially if she could work with a friend. One teacher made it a point to remark in an IEP that Thalia worked well with any student who was in her group.

Thalia began to use a variety of strategies in middle school to help reduce her anxiety. Thalia started to implement interim due dates for portions of an assignment when she was given a long-term homework project so that she did not feel overwhelmed in completing the task as the deadline approached. Another way that Thalia was able to better adjust to middle school was by observing her classmates. Thalia noticed some of the ways that other students dealt with school situations. Thalia used their behavior cues to help her transition to different activities and to help her keep up with the structure of the school day. The teachers found that Thalia's overall coping skills improved throughout the school year in sixth grade.

Another core class was introduced when Thalia had to take a required foreign language in seventh grade. Thalia chose Spanish. Thalia performed on grade level in Spanish class, as she did in all of her academic subjects in seventh grade. Thalia received in-class support for reading and language arts, social studies, and science in seventh grade. She received additional support services for math. A shared personal aide was once again assigned to Thalia.

Thalia continued to receive in-class support for science in eighth grade. She was now going to receive additional support services for math, reading and language arts, and social studies. There was certainly never an issue of Thalia failing a subject in either sixth or seventh grade. Getting a low grade for one marking period in those years was a rarity. It was still decided to provide this supplementary support.

Thalia had some difficulty in eighth grade. Thalia's grades for her first two marking periods in eighth grade were lower than in previous years. Thalia had an A in technology education, and she earned a B in her consumer science, physical education, and health classes. Thalia's performance in her core academic classes was the concern. Her grade in reading and language arts was a B– in both marking periods. She earned C+ grades in science. Her first marking period grade in social studies was a C before it improved to a C+. In math, however, Thalia's grade dropped from a C+ to a C. In Spanish, her grade dropped from a C+ to a C-.

Issues were emerging in Thalia's classes that were uncommon to how she performed in school. The social studies teacher noticed Thalia struggling to keep up with the pace of the class. There was a concern that Thalia could be disorganized at times, which contributed to her being confused about how to complete certain tasks. Thalia was again getting frustrated when she could not figure out what she had to do on an assignment. The science teacher encouraged Thalia to more frequently attend extra help sessions. The Spanish teacher reported that Thalia appeared to be listening during lectures, but that she was quiet in class. Thalia was not seeking help when she did not understand the material in that class. The Spanish teacher even indicated some skepticism that Thalia was putting forth the effort needed to do well. Other teachers never had an issue with Thalia's work habits in class. Her effort was consistently praised throughout her school years.

Another source of anxiety that emerged in middle school was that the class discussion topics were more serious in terms of tragic world events and societal problems. Thalia became agitated when her teachers or classmates were discussing topics of this nature.

Some of Thalia's teachers noticed that she became sad and frightened by some of these stories and the ideas that her classmates put forth. Lorena became aware of this fear as well. Thalia would ask Lorena general questions, such as why does evil exist? Or, why do people have to be mean to each other? Thalia needed an explanation of the event as well as the reassurance of the outcome that she was going to be safe to reduce her nervousness.

Thalia's eighth grade school experience was an indication of a lack of comfort and confidence in her environment. It was a result of her not being able to manage her stress as much as it was a sampling of her academic ability. Thalia's anxiety in eighth grade appeared to be manifesting itself more negatively than it had in the past. Thalia was struggling with how her disability was affecting her outlook on school and how she thought of herself.

CHAPTER 27

EIGHTH GRADE MEANT THAT THALIA HAD TO UNDERGO AN-
other comprehensive triennial review. In some ways, the
review came at an ideal time as this evaluation might reveal why
eighth grade was presenting many problems for Thalia. The review
could identify and offer answers to the challenges that Thalia was
experiencing that did not exist in previous school years. The outcome of this triennial review would be pivotal to Thalia's education
plan as she entered high school the following year.

The review was comprised of an evaluation of all of Thalia's
student records, including some of her actual assignments, teachers'
input, observations, and an interview with Thalia. The review took
place in February and March of her eighth grade year. Thalia was
still operating under a special education disability classification
of emotionally disturbed as the reason that made her eligible to
receive support services.

Thalia was observed in her reading and language arts class as part of the triennial review. Thalia was seated with three other students when the examiner entered the classroom. The examiner saw Thalia organizing her materials as she prepared for class. The examiner made a note that Thalia was wearing glasses. Information about that day's class was written on the board in different sections. There was a section with the heading, "Do Now." Thalia effortlessly completed the, "Do Now," in-class exercise. Thalia listened attentively with her eyes focused on the teacher as the previous night's homework was reviewed.

Another section written on the board was that day's class objective. The teacher gave instructions that the next segment of the class was for the students to go around the room and interview their classmates to gather information for an op-ed writing assignment. The students could interview the teacher as well. Thalia's op-ed topic was cyberbullying. The examiner witnessed Thalia dutifully going to several of her classmates, asking them questions, and writing down their responses. The examiner thought that Thalia was productive in listening to her classmates' opinions and collecting that information. The examiner felt that Thalia effectively completed what was required for that step of the op-ed essay assignment.

The final section written on the board was that upcoming night's homework assignment. The examiner spoke with Thalia's teacher after class where it was mentioned that Thalia approached the teacher and nervously asked questions about the details of that homework assignment. Thalia's teacher and the teacher's aide confirmed that Thalia sought clarification about concepts and directions. They also informed the examiner that it was noticeable that Thalia got uptight when she was unsure of an assignment's instructions.

The examiner found Thalia to be friendly during their interview.

Thalia was asked about school, her learning style, and her out-of-school recreational activities. Thalia said that she enjoyed reading. Thalia reported that she performed, "OK," in math, but that she did not like the subject. Thalia told the examiner that she did not like science, "at all," and that she liked social studies, "a little."

Thalia claimed that she, "knows her learning style." She described herself as a visual learner. Thalia told the examiner that she did not like making, "a big deal," about how she learns. She described her aide as, "a helper." Thalia later mentioned that she, "does not like the aide." This was not a statement about the individual person who served in the role of her aide. It was an emphatic plea that she did not like having an aide and that she did not want extra classroom help. Thalia told the examiner that she felt more like, "a regular student" in school when she was younger.

Thalia described her recreational activities as, "doing stuff with friends." She mentioned the activities that she did with her friends were: ice skating, listening to music, hiking, going to parties, and playing soccer. Thalia said that she was looking forward to beginning babysitting. She mentioned to the examiner that she was taking a babysitting class at the YMCA. Finally, Thalia identified fashion as an area of interest that she might pursue when she got older.

Thalia had to complete a series of tests designed to assess her skill in reading, written language, comprehension, and math. Thalia had to read short, simple sentences and decide if the statement was true. Thalia completed all of the questions with only two errors. Thalia had to read a short passage and identify a missing keyword that made sense in the context of the story in one of the reading comprehension tests. Thalia efficiently worked through this task. She silently read the passage and quickly provided an answer before moving on to the next item. She scored at the higher end of the average range on this task in comparison to others her age.

The most extensive language skill test measured Thalia's writing ability in expressing ideas, opinions, and thoughts in a creative and mature way. A picture prompt was provided. Thalia then had five minutes to plan a story and fifteen minutes to write it out. Thalia used four minutes to plan her story. She scribbled down phrases and notes on the setting, characters, and crafting a potential plot.

The examiner found Thalia's story introduction to be somewhat interesting. The plot was logical and there was a sequencing of events. The characters were found to show mild emotion. The storytelling was considered to be adequate. Thalia wrote for only nine of the fifteen minutes allowed. It was thought that the story could have been more fully developed if Thalia used all of the allotted time.

As for the writing, Thalia's spelling was excellent. She used the rules for capitalization and punctuation correctly. Thalia properly used quotation marks. Her story appropriately included exclamation points and question marks. Thalia's noun-verb agreement was correct. The words used in the story were thought to be well-selected. Thalia nicely used introductory phrases for some of her sentences. She effectively wrote one compound sentence. Thalia did write one run-on sentence and one fragment. She also did not write the story in paragraph form. Thalia's performance placed her in the superior range on the writing analysis task after assessing both the story plot and the writing.

Thalia stated to the examiner that she, "did not like math," as the math portion of the test was about to begin. Thalia performed well on addition, subtraction, and multiplication problems with single and multiple-digit numbers. She mistakenly added when she should have subtracted on one problem. Thalia was able to add and multiply negative numbers. Thalia had difficulty computing division problems. Thalia successfully solved fraction problems with the same denominator, but she struggled when the denominators were different.

Thalia underwent a psychological evaluation on March 2, 2011. The stated purpose of this evaluation was, "to determine if she continues to be eligible for special education and related services." Thalia was observed during lunch period as part of the psychological evaluation. Thalia sat at a lunch table with six female students. The conversation was ongoing and reciprocal. Thalia maintained eye contact when speaking to her friends. She was observed laughing at the other girls' comments throughout lunch. Thalia gave every indication that she was at ease and happy in this environment.

Thalia went to her locker after lunch to retrieve her books for Spanish class. She walked in the hallway with one of the friends whom she was seated with at lunch. Thalia continued to be observed as she organized the materials for the beginning of Spanish class and as the teacher gave a set of instructions to the entire class.

Thalia willingly participated in an individual assessment session with the psychologist. Thalia was attentive and focused during the evaluation. She sustained eye contact with the psychologist throughout their meeting. Thalia did ask the psychologist many questions. She wanted to know why she was being evaluated. Thalia asked about the requirements for taking honors classes in high school. Thalia told the psychologist that she was excited about high school. She particularly mentioned that she was looking forward to the elective classes that she signed up to take. Thalia had a fashion class and a ceramics class on her ninth grade schedule.

Thalia was attentive to the exercises that she was asked to

complete as part of the psychological evaluation. The examiner made a note that Thalia was taking the evaluation seriously. Thalia had to fill out a series of questionnaires. Thalia asked for clarification if she did not know the meaning of a statement on a questionnaire. Thalia carefully checked her work before submitting it to the psychologist to ensure that it was completed to the best of her ability.

Thalia reported that she shares positive relationships with her teachers. Thalia indicated her belief that the teachers care about her. Thalia admitted that she finds school to be boring at times, but that she does care about her grades. Thalia acknowledged that she is self-conscious about her intellectual ability.

Thalia rated herself on characteristics of social stress, anxiety, and depression. Thalia responded that she felt in control of her life and that she did not feel inadequate. Her sensation-seeking was common to those her age. Thalia remarked that she, "sometimes," forgets things and that she may occasionally have difficulty paying attention. Thalia responded, "often," to a question that asked if she experienced the feeling that she needs to get up and move around. She also responded, "often," to a question about talking without waiting for others to finish their thoughts.

Thalia filled out a questionnaire about her self-perceptions and self-esteem. Thalia had an overall positive perception of herself and her life. Thalia felt that she was attractive. She thought of herself as self-reliant. She believed that her school behavior as a whole was appropriate. Thalia reported having comfortable relationships with her peers. She thought that she was well-liked by her classmates. Thalia responded that her relationship with her family was positive.

Thalia's social and emotional characteristics were also assessed through an interview with the psychologist. There was some redundancy in the areas that she replied to on the questionnaires.

The interview allowed Thalia to express her thoughts and emotions about these areas in greater detail. Thalia displayed intense honesty about her situation in the interview.

Thalia again conveyed that she was concerned about her academic success. Thalia stated that she, "worries about grades and if they are good." Thalia added, "I wish I could be a smarter person." Thalia explained that her greatest fear in school was that her teachers might call on her in front of the class. The possibility of that happening increased Thalia's stress level. Thalia mentioned that she did not like giving oral presentations in the classroom.

Thalia expressed to the psychologist that she sometimes felt that her teachers, "don't get how hard it is for me." The psychologist encouraged Thalia to speak to her teachers about her concerns and to alert them to her fears that, until now, she largely kept private. The examiner thought telling the teachers might help Thalia alleviate her apprehension. Having an eighth grade student readily come forward to talk to a teacher about experiencing pressure and feeling tense was not easy. Thalia wondered if that teacher might think less of her. She thought that the teacher might perceive her inability to control her nerves as a sign of weakness.

The psychologist picked up on Thalia's signs of experiencing anxiety. The psychologist, however, determined that these emotions were not interfering with her acquisition of grade level material or her ability to make academic progress if she had minimal support. Thalia performed well on the academic tests that were part of the triennial review to support the psychologist's assessment.

Thalia's classroom performance in eighth grade might have led to the conclusion that she needed to retain or increase her education support services. Thalia's answers in some of the interviews as part of the triennial review were much more indicative of her true desires. Thalia saw the triennial review as an opportunity to tell her story and change the trajectory of her schooling. Thalia was clearly communicating during the review process that she did not want to have any classroom support. It was revealed during the evaluation that Thalia mentioned to her science teacher that she wanted to work on her own. This was an important admission by Thalia in expressing how she wanted to experience school.

Some special education students might feel comfort in having an aide with them. Thalia felt the complete opposite at this point in her life. The aide was an anchor in Thalia's mind. The aide removed Thalia's confidence. It was a reminder of a negative, that she had a disability. Having an aide, from Thalia's perspective, gave her the impression that she could not achieve. It was not allowing Thalia to fulfill her potential. Thalia desperately wanted to challenge herself.

Thalia showed her ambitious nature when asking the psychologist about honors classes in high school. Thalia also repeatedly mentioned that she looked forward to high school. She definitely did not want the stigma that might come from her classmates of being a high school student in special education classes and in need of an aide. Thalia had enough of people constantly hovering over her. Thalia also certainly did not want to enter high school with the classification of being emotionally disturbed that she had throughout middle school. Thalia craved a new beginning.

A conversation was started about Thalia going to high school without any education support services. The prominent characteristics of Thalia's academic performance and her social awareness reached a point where everyone knew what to expect. The positives were that Thalia had good study habits, always completed her homework on time, and she had a strong desire to achieve good grades. Teachers found Thalia to be consistently prepared for class. Thalia was a good citizen who followed the school and classroom rules and procedures. She was courteous to her peers and her teachers.

The negatives were that Thalia experienced anxiety when the learning material was difficult and when the answers to questions did not come quickly. Her haste in completing some assignments hindered her performance. She became frustrated and was not willing to accept suggestions that would improve her work. The teachers could better motivate Thalia as they got to understand her learning and behavior tendencies. Thalia's performance in the classroom improved when that occurred. Thalia's being comfortable and her belief that the teachers wanted her to succeed were what often made the difference.

The decision was to move forward in a bold way for high school with Thalia no longer having any support services. The sense was that Thalia could succeed if she was placed in the right setting and given the right course schedule. Having no services would be a major adjustment, combined with all of the other challenging aspects of beginning high school. Thalia was thrilled with the decision that she would not have services for the first time in her schooling. She saw it as an opportunity for independence and growth. Thalia told Lorena, "it is time, mom. I need to be on my own."

Donnie and Lorena came to understand that they needed to give Thalia this chance. Lorena was apprehensive about Thalia not having any support services. Thalia's receiving services was something that gave Lorena comfort as her daughter went through school. For Lorena, Thalia's having an individual aide meant that someone was always there to guide and help her. That person, that security, was no longer going to be there. Lorena particularly thought that support would be helpful in certain situations, such as having extra time to take a test. Lorena felt that Thalia accomplished so much, why alter the approach that was generally working? Lorena also had a concern about what if Thalia had a setback and support services needed to be re-introduced. How would Thalia handle that outcome? What stress and anxiety could that bring for Thalia?

Lorena spoke with Lisa about the decision to eliminate support services. Lisa thought that Thalia not having any services was worth trying. Lisa saw it as an opportunity to see how Thalia could perform when she was completely on her own. Donnie and Lorena would certainly remain vigilant about how Thalia was doing in school. They did not need an IEP or a child study team to make sure that Thalia was giving a good effort and that she was able to successfully complete her schoolwork.

CHAPTER 28

THALIA FELT CONFIDENT IN ENGLISH, SPANISH, AND HIS-tory classes throughout high school. She never regretted that she stopped having support services for those subjects. This sentiment was reflected in her grades. Thalia earned an A– in English in three of the four years in high school, with a B in her sophomore year. After a B in her freshman year in Spanish, Thalia earned a B+ in her sophomore and junior years. Thalia achieved a grade of a B in her freshman modern world history class, with a B+ in U.S. history in her sophomore year, and a B in her junior year.

Thalia, at times, did feel that some support services would have been helpful in her math classes. Thalia received a C in algebra one in her freshman year. Thalia's grade in geometry class as a soph-omore was a C-. It was still decided not to introduce any support services for math. Livingston created a section of intermediate algebra that was designed for students who had difficulty in math. The class was co-taught by a general education math teacher and a special education teacher. It was recommended to Thalia that she take this section of math rather than the more advanced algebra two class. Thalia was enrolled in the intermediate section of algebra in her junior year. She earned a grade of a B+. Thalia took a college math seminar class in her senior year, again earning a B+.

Science was another subject in which Thalia felt that some support services would have been helpful. She earned a C+ in biology as a freshman. She received a C in chemistry in her sophomore year, a class that has a great amount of math application. Thalia earned an A- in her junior year environmental science class.

The challenges for Thalia morphed from solely the academic issues related to her learning disability to include the growing up dilemmas that every other teenager confronts. These are the unavoidable difficulties of the social aspects of being in high school and the drama of those years that needed to be dealt with daily. The obstacles of being that age became more of a concern than the academic challenges that Thalia faced. Thalia was adequately handling her schoolwork. The fact that the social problems of a typical teenager became dominant could be thought of as a sign of progress. Yet, the demands of overcoming both the education and social dynamics of high school could be daunting while Thalia managed the traits of her disability.

Growing up in Livingston presented another challenge. Some families in town were wealthy. Thalia's classmates were wearing designer brands of clothes and drove expensive cars. Fitting in this environment could be difficult. Thalia was not materialistic. She generally did not feel peer pressure to act a certain way or possess a certain item. Thalia was her own person. She knew to act to her comfort level. Thalia always socially behaved a little older than her age. She thought that some of her high school classmates were immature. Thalia had a group of friends with whom she enjoyed spending time. Thalia had little interest in being part of the crowd that wanted to party, nor did she desire to be included in any particular high school social scene.

Lorena knew that high school could be a troublesome time in any person's life. She was aware that other students could make comments that were intended to be hurtful. Lorena told Thalia that if she ever got upset by something that her classmates said or did to not let them see her cry, to hold it in until she got home. Lorena told Thalia to not let the students bully her and that she had to stand up for herself if any of them tried. Thalia was comfortable with standing tall, looking another classmate in the eye, and speaking her mind back to that person if needed. Thalia was also willing to stand up for a friend whom she felt was being bullied.

Livingston High School had an enrollment of slightly less than two thousand students. Thalia's transition to high school began before the first day of classes. Thalia saw a flyer in middle school about trying out for the color guard team that was part of the Livingston High School band. Thalia attempted to convince some of her friends to try out for the color guard team as well, but she was not able to do so. Thalia was not deterred by having to join the team without knowing any of its other members. It was a moment of pure happiness for Thalia when she made the team and received her uniform. She was the only freshman on the color guard team.

Thalia worked hard to learn the skill of throwing an object up in the air and catching it. She practiced constantly on her own in the backyard. She first used a broomstick before practicing with the two different flags and the wooden rifle that she would use when the band performed. Thalia was also practicing all of the choreography that was required. Thalia never complained about the commitment that it took to be a member of the color guard team. The coaches enjoyed having Thalia on the team. They easily noticed and greatly appreciated her dedication.

Being part of the high school band offered Thalia an opportunity to socialize with other students outside of the classroom. Everyone on the color guard team, and the band as a whole, had a common purpose of giving a great performance and proudly representing the school. It provided Thalia with a sense of belonging and identity. Thalia's confidence was boosted.

The band provided Thalia with great structure for the hours outside of school. The band practiced three times per week, performed on Saturday when the high school football team played its games, and on Sunday there was often a band competition. The color guard team might do a show at other special events. The color guard team performed between the first and second periods of a New Jersey Devils hockey game at the Prudential Center arena in Newark on one occasion.

Donnie eagerly anticipated Thalia's first performance with the color guard at one of the high school team's football games. Donnie witnessed the effort that Thalia put in to do her best. He knew that Thalia never missed band practice. He also sensed how much Thalia was looking forward to the halftime show. He desperately wanted Thalia's dedication to be rewarded with a great day. Donnie was a bit nervous for his daughter, as any father would be. He thought, what if she dropped the flag? What if she threw the flag in the air and she did not catch it? Or, what if she threw the flag and it hit another member of the band? None of Donnie's worst fears materialized. Thalia was flawless in her performance. Donnie watched his daughter in complete amazement. He was incredibly impressed.

It was not until senior year that Thalia finally convinced two of her friends to join the color guard team. Thaila was named the captain of the team for her senior year. Thalia was responsible for teaching the routines to the younger team members. Thalia often invited her teammates over to her house to practice. Thalia enjoyed being a mentor. There was also the opportunity for the Livingston High School band to perform at Walt Disney World in Florida in her senior year. It was the first time that Thalia went away without Donnie and Lorena. Thalia had a wonderful trip with her friends and the band performed well.

All of the senior members of the band were introduced and acknowledged at the final home football game. It was a special moment for Thalia. It was gratifying for Donnie and Lorena to see Thalia participate in an activity for four years that brought her so much joy. Thalia was awarded the Livingston High School Band Booster Scholarship as a senior, "in recognition of your leadership, talent/skills, and dedication to the color guard program." She looked back at the entire experience with fondness and appreciation as it ended.

Thalia joined the Key Club as another high school activity. The Key Club was a community service group where the students volunteered to help with different events and organizations in town. The Key Club had meetings twice per month after school to discuss opportunities for reaching out to the community. Students had to volunteer a certain number of hours per month to be an active Key Club member.

Thalia most liked the activities that were meaningful to others. Thalia participated in the Key Club's visit to a local senior citizens' home. She worked the game tents at the Kiwanis organization's carnival. The Livingston Key Club hosted an intergenerational prom in the high school cafeteria where senior citizens were invited to interact with the students.

Thalia was dealing with other exciting aspects of being a teenager, such as learning to drive and beginning to work. Thalia passed the written driving exam in her sophomore year of high school. Thalia got her driving permit when she turned sixteen years old. It was the summer going into her junior year. Thalia was required to complete six hours behind the wheel with a driving school. Thalia was enthusiastic to learn to drive. She scheduled the first of her three, two-hour sessions with the driving instructor to occur on the day of her sixteenth birthday. It was the first day that she was eligible for lessons. Thalia would practice driving with Donnie and Lorena using their mini-van. The mini-van became Thalia's car to use after she passed the driving road test.

Thalia became interested in getting a job while in high school. She wanted the independence of having her own money. Thalia had been babysitting since she was fourteen years old. Thalia went and got her working papers when she turned sixteen for Donnie and Lorena to sign their approval. Lorena advised Thalia to be persistent and to continue calling when there was a job opening that she wanted.

Thalia got a job at a local clothing store in December 2013, her junior year in high school. It was another situation for Thalia to show that she was responsible and that she could effectively manage her time. Working in the clothing store provided Thalia with an excellent opportunity to interact with people. Thalia assisted customers in finding items throughout the store. She would suggest brands and outfits and help the customers make their merchandise selections. Thalia filled inventory and helped maintain the appearance of the store as her other duties. Thalia also took a job as a summer camp counselor at the YMCA, the same place where she attended swimming class when she was a child.

Lorena and Thalia often spent Saturday together during high school once the football season ended and the band members had that day free. Lorena would ask Thalia every day, "how was school?" That question rarely got a detailed response, typical of many teenagers. Saturday became Lorena's chance to bond and connect with her daughter, while Donnie worked. Lorena and Thalia began the day by going to the gym. They came home for a shower before going out to lunch. Thalia was opening up to Lorena during these mother/daughter days. Lorena started to learn about what was occurring in Thalia's life on a range of topics from issues at school, to relationships with boys, to her thoughts about world events. Their lunches became emotional at times.

Thalia began discussing her future plans with Lorena. Attending college was at the forefront of Thalia's thoughts. Thalia was contemplating what she might choose as a major in college. Livingston High School offered a variety of elective courses. Thalia took two years of fashion classes, a class in television production, and a creative photography class. Thalia enjoyed these subjects. She received an A in all of the classes, but none of them felt like a career.

Thalia thought about a career in physical therapy. She went to work with Lorena on occasion and she saw her mother perform the job as a physical therapist assistant. Thalia also participated in a one-week nursing camp while she was in high school at the hospital where Lorena worked.

Thalia considered psychology. She received an A in her psychology class in her junior year of high school. Thalia had to take a test to be enrolled in an advanced placement psychology class in her senior year. The students who did not pass the test had to maintain a grade of C or better or they would be dropped from the class. Thalia passed the test and she stayed in the advanced placement psychology class for the entire school year. She earned a B in the class.

Thalia then took the advanced placement psychology exam. Thalia scored high enough on the exam to earn three college credits. Thalia was able to use her high school psychology class to replace having to take that course in college. Thalia ultimately decided that there might be more schooling than she was willing to commit to at that time for her to choose psychology as a college major and career.

Thalia thought about speech therapy, having experienced many sessions throughout her education. Thalia was interested in the science and the learning techniques involved in getting children to improve their communication and reading skills. Thalia decided not to pursue speech therapy. It was becoming clear to Thalia that she wanted to have a career where she would help people, especially children.

Thalia took a part-time job in a preschool daycare center when she was sixteen years old because she wanted to get experience working with children. The daycare center was a bilingual preschool that taught children English, Spanish, and later added Chinese into its curriculum. Thalia worked at a couple of different daycare centers from her senior year of high school through her first couple of years of college. Thalia decided that she did not want to work with children who were that young, but she did find her time spent at the daycare centers to be valuable.

Thalia came to realize that she was comfortable and enjoyed being in an educational setting. Going to college to become a school teacher emerged as a natural career to pursue. Thalia felt inspired by the teachers who helped her. Frankly, she thought that she could do the job better than some of the teachers whom she had for class. Thalia was confident that she would perform the role of a school teacher in a very caring and supportive way.

Thalia had the opportunity to take a senior service class in the spring before graduating high school. The class was tailored for students who wanted a career in the education field. The seniors were placed at an elementary school in town where they performed the duties of a classroom aide. Thalia would leave high school early every day and work at the elementary school in the afternoon. Thalia was assigned to a first grade classroom. Thalia had to take pictures in the classroom and complete a daily journal documenting her experience for the senior service class requirements. Thalia liked being around children of this age. She started to think that working with the students in the younger grades of elementary school might be her desired age group to be a teacher.

Thalia applied to four universities: Iona College in New York, and Seton Hall University, William Paterson University, and Kean University in New Jersey. Thalia and her cousin, Deanna, visited Kean University together with their parents. Thalia took the SAT admissions exam without any special accommodations being that she no longer had an IEP to receive support services in high school.

The personal essay as a component of the college application process allowed Thalia to discuss what she experienced as a child with an autism diagnosis. Thalia described how she handled her disability and how it continued to shape her as a student and a person. Thalia offered some of what she had to endure and the emotions that resulted from those moments. Thalia wrote about her disability once for an assignment in English class. The personal essay on the college application was an occasion for Thalia to discuss her experience in her own words with an even greater level of detail, to people who did not know her at all. Thalia wrote:

> "Ok, Thalia, now repeat after me, 'the dog jumped over the puddle and splashed the little boy,'" the speech therapist stated. I gazed around the room and the cold white walls suffocated me on the inside. All I could hear was the perfect tone that came of her voice. It was the song of a bird on a warm summer's day. I grasped onto my own throat. It

occurred to me that I may never be able to make that sound. The smell of defeat filled the air as I puzzled over these words and phrases that were foreign to me. The saliva bubbles in my mouth as my struggle worsens and I begin to give up hope and face the reality that my disability will forever affect how I comprehend situations.

Fast forward to present day in algebra class. I feel overwhelmed with all of these formulas that are Egyptian hieroglyphics. The chilling sensation rolls down my back as the teacher explains the problem. "Thalia, what did you get for your answer?" My teacher asked. I was frozen like an iceberg. All I could see was a mixture of letters and numbers spread across the board. However, I was determined to figure out the answer, *but how?* The formula jumped in my head like a game of scrabble, just waiting for that epiphany moment. "The answer is … six," I whispered as I gulped down my fear. "Yes, that is correct," the teacher replied. A feeling of relief rushed throughout my body and I no longer had the irritating ringing in my ear.

Maybe I need to give myself more credit and have more confidence in myself. Maybe I am smarter than I think and I should praise myself on my strengths and not punish myself on my weaknesses. At the end of the day, it doesn't matter who you are or where you're from, no one's perfect and I am content with myself and that's all I could ask for. Living with a learning disability makes learning harder, but not impossible.

BANG! "Thalia, pay attention, we are going over your personal narrative assignment," my English teacher commanded. I used to be ashamed of who I was and my situation, but the moment I entered high school suddenly the opinions of others did not seem to affect me. I am fortunate enough to be surrounded by such amazing people in my life who accept me for the way I am and do not judge me on a daily basis. I was once asked the question if I had the opportunity to live my life without my learning disability, would I jump on that opportunity? Honestly, I wouldn't. My learning disability is what makes me different and I push myself every day to be a stronger person as a result of that. Perfection is an unrealistic ideal, however, happiness is a gracious gift that I am grateful to have.

Thalia was accepted to all four universities that she applied. With each acceptance came euphoric feelings of achievement and pride. She decided on Kean University because of its strong teaching program. A few of Donnie's cousins graduated from Kean's teaching program and they had been working in the field for many years. Kean University, located in Union, was also close to her house in Livingston.

Every high school student arrived on graduation day with a unique journey. For Thalia, fifteen years earlier she was in a doctor's office as her parents were being told that she had autism. Sorrow, fear, and uncertainty for Thalia's future were the predominant feelings on that day. Donnie and Lorena thought back to that moment and those emotions as Thalia walked across the stage and was handed her diploma.

CHAPTER 29

THALIA DECIDED TO COMMUTE THE TWENTY MINUTES FROM home to the Kean University campus for her freshman year. Thalia did not know anyone else who was attending Kean as she started college. One student whom she knew from Livingston High School did later transfer to Kean. The first class on her first day of college was statistics at nine o'clock in the morning. An intimidating subject for Thalia on an overall intimidating day. Thalia enrolled in a customary college load of five courses for her freshman fall semester. She also had to take a one-credit transition to Kean University freshman seminar. Aside from a C+ in her college composition class, Thalia earned an A or a B in all of her other courses. She ended the semester with a 3.25 grade point average.

Thalia decided to reduce her course load to four classes for her freshman spring semester. She intended to take one course over the summer. Thalia still had three credits from her high school advanced placement psychology class so there was no concern about her falling behind. Thalia had an outstanding spring semester. She earned three A's and one B. She was named to the Dean's List. Thalia received an A in her summer course. She completed her freshman year of college with a 3.52 grade point average.

There were some required classes that Thalia felt were a little pointless, a commonly held thought of many college students. Thalia genuinely enjoyed and appreciated the classes about her topics of interest. Thalia decided to double-major in education and sociology. Her first sociology class, the basic introduction to sociology course, was in the spring semester of her freshman year. She earned an A. Her first class in her education major was in the spring semester of her sophomore year. Thalia received an A in a course that focused on multicultural education settings.

Thalia enjoyed college much more than high school. She adjusted well to the independence of college. Thalia was responsible with the extra free time that comes with a college schedule of not being in class all day, every day. The transition from middle school into high school meant less hovering over Thalia from a teacher's aide when her special education services stopped. The transition from high school into college brought a greater level of freedom. Many people in college were not aware of Thalia's disability. Thalia could meet people and she would not immediately be judged by someone based primarily on her condition.

There were aspects of college that created some stress. Each semester's classes meant having to deal with different professors, along with new course material. Each semester's schedule was adjusted as well as the classes that Thalia had to take met at different days and times. Thalia's desire for structure persisted. There was a change to her daily routine every few months in college.

Thalia felt a bit overwhelmed at the start of every college semester. She wondered if she would know anyone in her new classes. She questioned if she could complete the course requirements and get good grades. Thalia would see all of the assignments for the entire semester and tell Lorena, "I cannot do this," and, "this is too hard." Lorena could almost predict when the beginning of the semester panic speech from Thalia was about to occur. Lorena would jokingly say to Donnie, "here it comes, any day now, Thalia is going to tell us that she cannot handle college."

It was always a brief moment of feeling tense rather than the reality that she would not be able to do well in her classes. Lorena would be able to calm her daughter and offer her the desired encouragement. Lorena constantly reminded Thalia that she and Donnie were there to help her in any way that she needed. Thalia settled in and performed well as the semester went along and she realized that all of her assignments were not to be finished at one time and that she had the ability to complete what was being asked. The strategies that Thalia used in high school of giving a dedicated effort, being organized, and completing assignments in smaller sections at time intervals before the final due date were once again used to help her navigate a college semester.

Thalia decided to live in an apartment near campus with three other female students for the fall semester of her sophomore year. Thalia would come to prefer living at home. She thought of leaving the apartment and moving back home at one point during the fall semester. Donnie and Lorena reminded Thalia that she made a commitment to her roommates. Donnie and Lorena encouraged Thalia to stick it out and learn from the experience. Thalia decided to once again commute to college when the semester was over. While Thalia gained life lessons from having the responsibility of living on her own, moving back home allowed her to eliminate some distractions and better focus on her schoolwork.

Students with special education needs can register with the

university disability office upon entering college. These students are provided with a document that they present to their professors at the beginning of each semester that details their needed accommodations for the class. These support services might include extra time on tests or assignments, taking tests in a less distracting environment, or having a classmate assist them with taking notes during lectures. Many students might not ever use the accommodations that they can receive. However, registering with the disability office and informing their professors of their situation offers the students the protection of executing these support services if needed. Thalia decided that registering with the Kean University disability office was not necessary after her experience of not having any support services in high school.

Math continued to be the subject that presented the greatest difficulty. Thalia was struggling with her college algebra course in the fall semester of her sophomore year. She had been enrolled in an intermediate-level section of algebra in her junior year of high school instead of algebra two. The algebra course in college was taught as if all of the students had a regular section of the class in high school.

The college algebra course met three times per week for fifty minutes. Thalia had trouble finishing the tests in a fifty-minute time period. There were distractions during a test as when other students finished, they would be gathering their things and leaving the classroom. Thalia would start to become preoccupied with looking at the clock and noticing that the time to complete the test was quickly vanishing. Thalia had to rush to simply finish a test. Thalia's early semester test scores were low. It reached the point where Thalia received an early warning letter that she was in danger of failing the course.

Thalia became nervous. Dropping the course would not solve the problem as she had to complete this curriculum requirement to graduate. Thalia was putting in the time and effort that she felt was needed to succeed in the course. She also thought that her understanding of the algebra concepts, while challenging, was not the problem. It was her inability to perform on the tests with the time constraint that was the cause of her low grades.

Thalia was comfortable advocating for herself when necessary. She decided to meet with the professor during office hours. Thalia explained to the professor that math was a difficult subject for her. Thalia informed the professor that she had education support services in the past, especially for math. She described the math courses that she took in high school. Thalia communicated to the professor that she believed that she was learning the subject material in class. Thalia plainly stated that completing the tests in fifty minutes was presenting a problem. Thalia told the professor that she believed that her test grades would improve if she had more time to finish.

The professor was understanding and accommodating of Thalia's needs. The professor agreed to allow Thalia extra time to complete the tests. Thalia would also take the tests in the professor's office where there would be fewer distractions. The new system worked. Thalia's test scores improved. She passed the class with a C. The sophomore algebra class was the second C of her college career. It was the last time that she received a grade that low in a class. College algebra was the only course that presented challenges to the extent that Thalia felt compelled to inform a professor of her autism spectrum diagnosis.

Thalia finished the semester with a 3.29 grade point average. She had an overall grade point average of 3.45. Thalia returned to being named to the Dean's List in the spring semester of her sophomore year. She would have just two classes where she received a grade lower than an A for the rest of her college career.

Thalia earned a 4.0 grade point average in the fall semester and a 3.8 grade point average in the spring semester of her junior year. Thalia's cumulative grade point average jumped to 3.64 after her junior year. The fall semester of her senior year was her second with a 4.0 grade point average. It was her fourth consecutive semester of being named to the Dean's List. Thalia had straight A's in the spring semester of her senior year. The sole requirement that remained for graduation in her education major was doing her student teaching.

A student who completes sixty college credits is eligible to substitute teach in New Jersey schools. Thalia put her name on the substitute teaching list in three school districts near her house. Thalia began getting called regularly to substitute teach on the days that she did not have her own college classes to attend. Thalia substituted at a high school on one occasion. She did not enjoy that environment. Thalia immediately knew that teaching at that level was not what she wanted to do. Most of her substitute teaching assignments were at an elementary school. A few of them did occur at a middle school.

Thalia confirmed for herself that working with younger, elementary school-aged children was her desire. Thalia made early childhood education her teaching specialty. Thalia also decided that she did not want to pursue a special education certification. Thalia wanted to teach in a general education classroom.

Thalia received her student teaching placement in a first grade class in the Union school district. Ironically, it was the same school where she attended kindergarten. It was the same school that Thalia left after one year when Donnie and Lorena felt that she was not getting the education and behavior support services that she needed. Thalia did not remember much of kindergarten or living in Union so returning to that school was not an emotional event in any way. Thalia was simply focused on doing the best that she could in her student teaching experience.

Thalia graduated from Kean University Magna Cum Laude. She had a final grade point average of 3.72. Thalia completed the certification requirements for a double degree in early childhood education, pre-kindergarten through third grade, and elementary education, kindergarten through sixth grade. She also graduated meeting the requirements for a sociology major. Thalia received an A in all twelve of her sociology courses.

Lorena and Thalia shared another poignant moment while she was in college. Lorena wanted Thalia to understand all that she had been through in confronting her autism diagnosis. Lorena pulled out a large box that contained all of the documents that she saved related to Thalia's disability. Lorena showed Thalia the pediatric neurologists' reports that detailed her behavior symptoms. Thalia was able to read what was said in those early visits about her future possibilities. Thalia also got to read two years of daily journals from the DLC, her report cards, and all of her IEP reports that had comments from her teachers. Thalia was a bit overwhelmed. Thalia did not remember anything from her younger years. She did recall moments from the upper grades of elementary school and middle school. Thalia looked at the large pile of papers and asked Lorena, "why did you keep all of this?"

Lorena thought that it was important for Thalia to know what it took for her to get to this point in her life. Lorena wanted her daughter to have a feeling of pride and appreciation for all that she achieved. The accomplishment of graduating college was far from a certainty for Thalia when she was a young child. One of Lorena's thoughts upon hearing Thalia's autism diagnosis at her first pediatric neurologist appointment was if Thalia would be able to attend college.

Lorena did not want Thalia to think of her disability as a negative, but rather as something that shaped her into the person that she grew to be. Lorena explained to Thalia that sometimes people have to go through challenging times to fulfill their potential. She wanted Thalia to have the confidence that nothing is holding her back from all that she wanted to achieve in the future. Thalia demonstrated that she can endure difficult moments. Thalia showed her ability to work hard and persevere to overcome her disability.

Lorena wanted Thalia to be more aware of all of the people who never gave up on her and sacrificed to give her a better life. Lorena explained to Thalia some of the conflicts with school administrators and how she and Donnie had to fight to get her all of the support services that she needed. She told Thalia the story of why their family moved to Livingston. Lorena described to Thalia how everyone in the family helped her. Lorena detailed how Lisa came to work with her every day in that initial summer. Lorena told Thalia of the efforts of her grandparents in watching her as she and Donnie went to work. Lorena described to Thalia that her aunts constantly brought her cousins over to the house to play with her and help improve her social skills.

Lorena also talked to Thalia about the responsibility that she was going to have as a school teacher. Lorena interacted with Thalia's teachers much more frequently than the parents of children who did not have special needs. Lorena had a unique and informed perspective of the parent/teacher relationship. Lorena wanted Thalia to understand that she would soon have the role of someone who needed to be compassionate, patient, and dedicated to the success of the young children who will be in her class. Thalia took all of what Lorena was telling her to heart. Thalia sensed how meaningful it was for Lorena to have this conversation. It was the latest valuable lesson from her mother.

CHAPTER 30

THALIA WENT ON A COUPLE OF INTERVIEWS FOR A TEACHING job and she felt that they went well. She was invited for a second interview to do a teaching demonstration for some of the openings. Yet, no offer materialized for a permanent teaching position. Thalia was offered a maternity-leave replacement position for a third grade class. The short-term role would start in March and go through the end of the school year in June. The position was not ideal because it was temporary, but Thalia was thrilled to have her own class. Thalia was in the classroom for one week when in-person learning was shut down because of the coronavirus pandemic. The remainder of the school year was virtual.

While Thalia was seeking to secure a teaching position, and just prior to her starting the temporary role, Lorena's cousin, Cecilia, mentioned that there was a shortage of school teachers in the surrounding communities where she lived in Virginia. Cecilia informed Thalia about a job fair for teachers that was taking place.

Thalia decided to visit Cecilia and attend the job fair. Thalia did preliminary interviews with a few school districts. More in-depth interviews with some of those school districts soon followed. Thalia started researching the towns in Virginia. She was getting excited about the opportunity to live in a new state, meet new people, and have a permanent teaching job.

Thalia received an offer from two school districts. Thalia was given the option to decide between two positions in the school district that first offered her a job. Thalia accepted the offer to teach a second grade class. Thalia was ecstatic when she was officially hired. She was now moving to Virginia to begin her teaching career. Thalia had two months from when she received her offer letter on May 28, 2020, to find an apartment and get settled in Virginia.

Moving to Virginia was a major decision. Thalia might obsess over a decision that she had to make. This characteristic may have been a residual effect of her disability or just her personality. Thalia would call Lorena to talk through an issue. It might seem to be resolved by the end of the call and a decision about how to proceed was made. Thalia would call Donnie a short time later, especially if she knew that her mother was not home, and talk through the same issue with him. Thalia felt more comfortable moving forward with a decision when the advice from both her mother and father was the same.

Donnie and Lorena knew how incredibly important moving to Virginia was for Thalia when they saw how easily she made that decision. Donnie and Lorena were supportive of Thalia's decision, despite it being difficult to not see their daughter every day. They did feel comfortable that Thalia was moving to a nice, safe community. Plus, Cecilia would be in the area. The four-hour drive made it so that weekend visits were manageable. Face-time and zoom calls made communicating with Thalia easier while she lived at a distance as well.

Donnie and Lorena could see that Thalia was excited as she prepared to leave for Virginia and start her teaching job. Donnie and Lorena knew that Thalia deserved this opportunity after witnessing everything that she experienced and overcame. They understood why Thalia wanted to leave New Jersey and get a fresh start at a place where nobody was aware of all that she had been through. It was a new beginning for Thalia where she could do things her way. Moving to Virginia in some aspects was Thalia's response to all of the years of being monitored and hovered over. The move meant no supervision. It brought unbridled freedom.

The start of the Virginia school year was pushed back until the end of August as the coronavirus pandemic continued to prevent in-person learning. The delay gave Thalia more time to plan her class lessons for the early weeks of the school year. It was decided that school would be virtual from August through late October. Thalia held online open house meetings with her students' parents to introduce herself and to get them more comfortable with the virtual form of learning.

A hybrid system was used starting in October. Half of the class attended school in person two days per week and the other half of the class was in person two other days. The entire class was virtual on Friday. This hybrid system lasted until April when classes started meeting in person four days per week. The classes were able to remain with in-person learning through the end of the school year.

Thalia was self-aware of executing her duties as a teacher. Thalia understood that the children in the class were her priority. Thalia decided that she would decline to take on extra work so that she could maintain her focus on teaching her class, such as leading school clubs. Thalia understood that she could become overwhelmed if she took on too much work. Thalia felt compelled to mention to some of the other teachers that she was diagnosed on the autism spectrum when she was younger. Thalia wanted them to know that she was not being disrespectful when she turned down participating in an extracurricular school activity.

Thalia was confronted with something that she knew all too well in her first year as a teacher, students who had learning and behavioral disabilities. Thalia had three children in her class who were diagnosed as being on the autism spectrum. Thalia had one teacher's aide in the class with her at all times. Each student displayed a different set of behaviors, but had a level of functioning that justified their placement in a general education classroom.

One boy was high functioning. This boy's noticeable symptoms were that he would become nervous, get out of his seat, and sometimes twirl in a circle when his routine was disrupted or when he was asked to complete a task that he did not want to do. He might exhibit these anxious behaviors when the learning topic changed from something that he enjoyed. There might be a math skill that he was interested in and wanted to continue practicing. He became irritated when the switch was made to the next skill that he was not yet sure about. The boy had an intense preoccupation with the solar system. He loved to draw pictures of the planets as his stimulating activity. His obsession made it so that sometimes paying attention to other subjects was difficult.

Another boy was very quiet. He spoke only in short phrases. His other communication tendency was to repeat himself. The boy never interrupted class. His academics were low. He had to copy the information that the teacher's aide wrote to help him understand an assignment's instructions.

One other boy was more vocal. He would scream and throw

things when he did not get his way. His behavior could be disruptive to the class. The classroom teacher's aide had to spend a great amount of time with this child. The teacher's aide would have to take him out of the classroom on occasion, making the aide unavailable to assist the other two children with special needs.

Thalia was patient with all of the children in her class, but especially with those who had learning disabilities. Thalia was also sensitive to the situation of her students with special needs when interacting with their parents. Thalia was now attending IEP meetings. Her observations and assessments regarding the students with disabilities were greatly impacting their education. Thalia would talk to Lorena about what was occurring with the students in her class. Thalia valued her mother's advice about some of the more challenging issues, particularly how to speak to a child's parents.

Thalia's first-year teaching evaluation conducted by the school's administrators found that she was effective in all seven areas that were assessed: professional knowledge, instructional planning, instructional delivery, assessment of and for student learning, learning environment, professionalism, and student academic progress. Thalia's dedication toward her students with special needs was highlighted in her teaching evaluation report. It was written that Thalia, "is a hard worker who works to understand her students' needs. She has also served as a collaborative teacher for several students in our autism program. Her co-teachers have shared with administration how much they appreciate her efforts and the way she supports their students."

Thalia also began graduate school in her first year of having a teaching job. Thalia enrolled in an online program through the University of Texas of the Permian Basin to get her master's degree in English second language education, with a minor in education leadership. The master's degree program consisted of twelve courses. Each course ran for eight weeks.

The online program was largely self-paced. The students did not have any regularly scheduled live classes with the professors. The course material and assignments were posted through an online platform in which Thalia reviewed the lectures and completed the assignments. Thalia especially enjoyed the cultural diversity course that was included in the English second language major and the education leadership course that was included in her minor. Thalia scheduled her courses so that she would complete her graduate degree in two years.

CHAPTER 31

THE VIRGINIA SCHOOL YEAR BEGAN AS SCHEDULED IN EARLY
August for Thalia's second year as a teacher. It was Thalia's
first year of completely in-person classes, with no virtual instruction planned (school was able to remain with in-person learning for
the entire year). Thalia quickly realized that most of the children
in her class were behind in their academics after a year and three
months of schooling through the combination of in-person and virtual learning. Thalia spent time reading with each of her students
early in the school year to assess their skill levels. She became very
concerned about one boy whose academics were far below the other
children. The boy was reading at a low level. Thalia could easily
see that the boy needed a great amount of time and assistance with
his reading. He also had trouble writing sentences and finishing
assignments. The boy showed decent math skills. He presented no
behavior issues and he got along well with his classmates.

Thalia strongly believed that this student would benefit from support services that focused on reading and writing improvement. Thalia initiated the process of getting the boy services by speaking with the school's vice principal. Thalia understood that it would take time before any services were started so she did not feel that she could delay raising her concerns. The lengthy process was a point of frustration for Thalia. She knew from her own experience how crucial it was to provide early intervention on the education support services that a child needs. Thalia was well aware that these learning problems become worse if they are not addressed. Thalia collected some of the boy's work and she showed it to the vice principal to demonstrate his immediate need for services. Thalia convinced the vice principal to conduct a meeting with the boy's family.

A meeting with the boy's father was held in September, one month into the school year. The meeting was attended by Thalia, the vice principal, a school psychologist, and the educational diagnostician. This group became the boy's child study team. Thalia began the meeting by expressing her concern and detailing some of the deficiencies in the boy's academic skills. She used the examples of the boy's work to support her claims. The boy's father was eager to begin support services for his son after hearing Thalia's presentation and the subsequent discussion with the child study team. He wanted to have any evaluation that was needed to make his son eligible for services to begin as soon as possible.

The child study team scheduled to reconvene in November for another assessment meeting. It was decided to have Thalia first try some in-class interventions. Thalia grouped the students in her class by their reading level. One in-class intervention that Thalia tried was to have reading exercises targeted to each group's needs. In addition to the reading lessons that she conducted with the entire class, Thalia read with those who were reading above grade level an extra once per week. Thalia read with the students who were reading at grade level an extra twice per week. She read with the students who needed the most help an extra three times per week. The students in the lower reading group were focusing on their pacing and sounding out words.

The school instituted a phonics program to help the students catch up with their reading skills after the instability of the previous school year. The teachers were asked to identify the students who needed the most help in this area. Thalia put the boy's name on the list to receive phonics assistance for twenty minutes every day. Thalia had a teacher's aide in the class who worked with the boy on his reading and phonics skills as well. Thalia also kept a close eye on the boy, offering him extra help when she could.

Parent-teacher conferences were held for each student in October. Thalia met with the boy's father and they discussed his son's academic situation. The boy's father again indicated that he was hoping that his son soon received education support services. Thalia explained to him that she was advocating for that outcome. She described a bit more about the process that was occurring to make that happen. Thalia explained all of the in-class intervention strategies that she was using to help the boy improve his reading. The boy's father greatly appreciated Thalia's efforts and compassion.

The child study team met with the boy's father in November to update his son's case. Thalia again presented samples of the boy's work as evidence that he needed assistance. The outcome of this meeting was that a comprehensive evaluation would take place to see if the boy qualified for special education services. The boy was to be evaluated in class, undergo a psychological evaluation, and all assessments of his work by Thalia would be provided. Thalia filled out multiple forms that highlighted the boy's strengths and weaknesses. Other members of the child study team did the same after their observations. It was an evaluation process that Thalia was extremely familiar having been through it when she was a young child. Thalia could remember her comprehensive review process in fifth and eighth grade.

A meeting was scheduled for February where the results of the evaluation process would be discussed and the boy's special education support eligibility finally determined. It was yet another two-month delay in starting services. Thalia continued to do as much extra work as she could with the boy during this time period.

The child study team met for ninety minutes in early February. Thalia explained that all of the in-class interventions that were used did not produce the desired improvement. Thalia indicated that these intervention strategies were helpful, but they were not sufficient. Thalia again detailed the boy's struggles with reading and writing. Thalia described that it took the boy a long time to read a paragraph or to get through a story. Thalia discussed that he was able to speak his thoughts, but that it was difficult for him to try to put those thoughts into words and form a coherent, organized sentence. She pointed out how the boy would get upset and frustrated when having to complete a writing assignment. Thalia explained that she did not want the boy's frustration tendencies to fester and become a more permanent personality trait that carried over into other aspects of his life.

Thalia spoke of the boy's troubles with paying attention and maintaining focus. Thalia reported that the boy had good social skills and that he interacted well with the other children. She also indicated that his motor skills were well-developed. Thalia was professional in her presentation, but it was an emotional moment for her. She understood what was at stake and the magnitude of the decisions that would be made at the conclusion of this evaluation process.

The child study team assessed that the boy was indeed eligible to receive support services. The boy's father and mother were both at this meeting which informed them of the child study team's decision. They were happy and relieved with the outcome. The school's lead special education teacher was to write up an IEP that detailed the specific support services that the boy was to receive. The IEP would be presented at another meeting at the end of February. The boy would immediately start with his special education services at that time.

The IEP established that the boy was to receive one hundred fifty minutes of reading instruction and one hundred minutes of language arts instruction from the special education teacher each week. He was pulled out of class every day to meet with the special education teacher in a small group setting. Thalia was relieved that the boy was a willing participant in receiving support services. He happily went with the special education teacher who came to the classroom to get him. Thalia could relate to the boy in knowing that it was not easy for a child to be singled out in this way in front of all of his classmates. The boy also received small group testing support on all state or district standardized testing. This IEP carried through to the third grade. Another meeting would be held to assess the boy's progress and determine if any adjustments to his education plan were needed at that time.

For Thalia, the outcome of the boy receiving special education support services was very personal and meaningful. Thalia was proud that she took the initiative to start the process to help the young boy and that she was such a fierce advocate for him. It was a rewarding validation of all that she went through on her journey as a child on the autism spectrum to get to the point where she could now have a tremendous impact on the life of a child who also had a learning disability.

As the boy's parents thanked her for all that she did, Thalia gained a new perspective on what Donnie and Lorena had to endure to get the proper education support services that she needed growing up. Thalia could appreciate the sacrifices of her parents in a way that she had not before. The young boy now had a greater hope for his future. Thalia now had a greater feeling of satisfaction, of a journey filled with purpose.

EPILOGUE

I T WAS NOTED IN THALIA'S PERFORMANCE REVIEW WHEN SHE finished her second year as a teacher that she, "made thoughtful contributions" to the IEP process for her students. Thalia was pleased to see that her extensive efforts toward helping the young boy were recognized. Thalia completed her master's degree that spring as well. She graduated with a 4.0 grade point average.

Thalia's disability is not something that she considers dealt with, but rather is something that she continues to confront in different ways, in different situations. Thalia understands that she has a life-long condition. She does not believe that her disability is completely eliminated or that it can be thought of as cured. What Thalia gained over the years is the ability to better manage her disability. She learned and applies techniques for improved social skills and how to be a better communicator. Thalia still desires structure and organization. She figured out how to adapt, be less rigid, and not easily become frustrated.

Thalia possesses an enviable self-awareness. She acts to her comfort level. Thalia then has personal work habits that have led to her success. Thalia began her schooling when she started working with Lisa. The early years of school, in particular, were very intensive. Putting a great amount of time and effort into what she is trying to accomplish is all that she knows. Thalia has a tireless desire to fulfill her potential. She is driven by wanting to make a significant difference in the lives of others.

There was much that Thalia had to endure and overcome. Thalia had to confront her thought of having to go to "stupid class" when she had to take math in the resource room in elementary school. Thalia pointedly told a school psychologist who was evaluating her in eighth grade that she sometimes felt that her teachers, "don't get how hard it is for me." Thalia had to display her courage to indicate to school administrators, and her parents, that she no longer wanted support services as she entered high school. It was her perseverance that helped her through other challenging situations in high school and college. All of Thalia's attributes were needed so that she was not defeated by her autism disability, but she allowed it to shape her only in a positive way. Every experience that Thalia had is what makes her the strong, independent, and confident woman that she is today.

Thalia knows the dedicated support that she received from her family. Thalia learned the value of working hard and how to approach challenges just by observing the example and listening to the guidance of her parents. Thalia is well aware of the sacrifices that Donnie and Lorena made and the moments of great difficulty that they too had to endure every time that she struggled.

Donnie and Lorena never lost focus on what Thalia needed to deal with her disability. Their relationship was strengthened by having to come together to support each other and to make sure that they did not let Thalia give up on herself. Donnie and Lorena were clear that Thalia understand that she could accomplish all that she desired.

Donnie and Lorena celebrated their twenty-eighth wedding anniversary in 2023. They live in the same house in Livingston, New Jersey that they moved to for their daughter to be in a school district that they believed provided her with the educational services that she needed. Donnie and Lorena know that they are incredibly blessed for all of the family support that they and Thalia received.

Family is certainly at the center of this story for Lisa. It was at her grandmother's seventy-seventh birthday party in December 1999, that Lisa first noticed and became concerned about Thalia's behavior. Lisa's priority was to help Thalia flourish academically and have a life filled with achievement and happiness. The situation provided a sense of purpose for Lisa. It was beyond personal for her. Yes, Thalia was her young cousin, but Lisa saw her in an even more meaningful way. Thalia was her cousin's daughter and her grandmother's great-granddaughter. At stake for Lisa was not letting down her family members when they needed her most. Any notion of their disappointment was enough of a motivation for Lisa to devote all of the time and energy that she could to help Thalia.

Grandma Morsillo was selfless. She taught everyone in her family to be there for one another. Lisa felt an emotional connection in helping Thalia. Grandma Morsillo might not have known all of the intricacies and challenges of an autism diagnosis, but she was well aware of Lisa's role in Thalia's life. Lisa cherished when her grandmother would say in her beautiful Italian accent, *"I know you are helping Thalia. Thank God for you, Lisa."*

Lisa entered into a career that she had not planned. It ended up being one of great passion. Her recognizing Thalia's symptomatic behaviors and working with Thalia five days a week for several hours every day conducting therapy began to shape Thalia's journey. Lisa was then offering guidance to Donnie and Lorena at many other points as well. Lisa assisted in getting Thalia into the DLC, attended many IEP meetings with Lorena, and recommended to Donnie and Lorena that they move to a new town.

Lisa continues to teach children with autism. The demand for trained professionals who work with children on the autism spectrum remains high. The number of children being diagnosed continues to demonstrate the magnitude of the problem. The United States Centers for Disease Control published a 2023 Community Report on Autism that found that based on 2020 data, one in thirty-six children is affected by autism. Boys are four times more likely than girls to be diagnosed with autism.

Autism Speaks, the charitable organization committed to the fight against autism, explains that it, "is dedicated to promoting solutions, across the spectrum and throughout the life span, for the needs of people with autism and their families." This mission recognizes that there are emergent issues that families, and society as a whole, have to confront in dealing with autism. One of the issues is when children who were diagnosed with autism move into adulthood. Education and related support services in the state of New Jersey end when a person reaches the age of twenty-one. The opportunities for employment or to learn new skills and be equipped to handle certain responsibilities are a challenge. There are also worries about co-occurring health conditions for those with autism as they get older. For the young children recently diagnosed with autism, determining the effects of the coronavirus on their education and social behavior development will need to be monitored and researched for years to come.

Lisa continues to advocate for teaching children through the principles of applied behavior analysis. The applied behavior analysis teaching method generally remains the most research-supported approach for improved learning and behavior outcomes for children with autism. Applied behavior analysis-based education is spreading to various teaching settings. These principles are being effectively implemented in classrooms with non-disabled students. Applied behavior analysis principles are also being used to condition other healthy behaviors, including quitting smoking and weight loss.

Someone has to notice the alarming behaviors of a child so that there is an impetus to have an evaluation by a pediatric neurologist, as Lisa did with Thalia. Parents have to know the age-appropriate behaviors of a child. They have to be vigilant in looking for the signs of autism symptomatic behaviors. A child's inability to communicate, deficient play and social skills, and any self-stimulating behaviors should all be cause for concern. Parents cannot be in denial or display a willingness to accept alternate explanations for what might be a life-altering disability. Parents cannot think that a child's peculiar behaviors are simply a phase. Parents have to be proactive, especially considering the consistent research-supported findings of the value of early intervention therapy.

Time is a critical element of an autism diagnosis and treatment. It is a beneficial resource when it is used properly, such as starting treatment as soon as possible and dedicating hours of therapy to a child. Time is a detriment to the treatment of autism when it is wasted, such as a family waiting to see if a child's concerning behaviors dissipate, delay in having an appropriate medical assessment, or use ineffective, non-research-supported treatment methods. A child is brought to see a doctor when sick with a fever. It should be the same mindset of being evaluated when alarming behavior symptoms are present. The assessment for autism or other behavior disorders is non-evasive. It is responding to questions and the child is observed. The burden of cost for treatment has been somewhat lessened with all fifty states passing laws that insurance companies have to provide coverage for applied behavior analysis therapy.

Today, Lisa works for a New Jersey school district where she consults with classrooms for students with disabilities utilizing the principles of applied behavior analysis. Lisa is also the founding director of Motivating Change, an agency that provides behavior consultation. Lisa and Rich celebrated their twentieth wedding anniversary in 2023. They live in Pennsylvania with their two daughters, Haidyn and Callie.

Lisa describes Thalia's improvement as, "we got to her brain at the right time. She was ready to learn." Why Thalia was inflicted with autism will forever be a mystery. What is not as mysterious in attributing to Thalia's improvement is the amount and level of treatment that she received. The combination of early intervention in starting Thalia with therapy before she was three years old, the number of hours of one-on-one daily therapy in that initial summer, her schooling for the next two years at the DLC, and Lorena constantly working with her daughter provided the treatment that Thalia needed in those early years. Thalia then had to put in all of the time and hard work that was required throughout her education. Thalia's grandfather, Dan, refers to her overcoming the challenges of her disability and her successes as a, "miracle of effort."

On July 17, 2021, Maria Morsillo passed away at the age of ninety-nine. Maria and her husband, John, were married in 1940 when she was eighteen years old. John passed away from a heart attack in December 1972. It was nine months after Lisa was born in March. Lisa often thought about her grandfather when she worked with Thalia. Lisa was seemingly hoping for some divine guidance as she helped his great-granddaughter. Grandma Morsillo, who lived her life for others, had a request upon her death – all donations in her memory be made to help in the fight against autism.

Three generations of the Morsillo family gathered at Tricia's house for dinner the night before Grandma Morsillo's funeral. Lisa had the same feeling of amazement that she always got when she saw Thalia. It was on that day that Donnie, Lorena, and Lisa once again reminisced about all that Thalia went through and celebrated all that she accomplished. Every great moment of achievement for Thalia brought back a vivid reminder of where she was years earlier. Donnie, Lorena, and Lisa know that what enabled Thalia's story to occur will not be the same for all other children. Each child's situation has different variables. Some children are obviously on the more severe end of the autism spectrum. It is often noted in the research studying autism treatments that there are no guarantees of improved behavior outcomes if receiving therapy.

There, however, are similarities between Thalia's story and that of other children on the autism spectrum that Thalia, Donnie, Lorena, and Lisa thought could be shared. The intention of telling Thalia's journey was to offer insight into the experiences, the emotions, the challenges confronted, the sacrifices demanded, and the decisions needed to be made at different stages of a child's life. Thalia, Donnie, Lorena, and Lisa believe that telling this story might help families navigate the obstacles of dealing with autism and offer them some hope.

Donnie concedes that Thalia's journey could have turned out vastly different at so many points. It was three years before Thalia was born that Lisa had what at the time was a random conversation with her friend, Stephanie, who invited her to visit the DLC. That singular conversation presented a defining moment for Lisa, one more impactful than she realized at that time.

Of course, what would have happened if Lisa did not see

two-and-a-half-year-old Thalia at her grandmother's birthday party? Thalia was not going to miraculously get better. Her alarming behaviors would have gotten increasingly worse in all likelihood. When would Thalia's situation have been noticed and addressed? Perhaps, once Thalia reached elementary school a concerned teacher might have been proactive in indicating that there was a problem, as Thalia did with the young boy in her class. Might the prime period for true improvement for Thalia have been missed?

Finally, there was the moment of Thalia receiving an autism diagnosis. Three pediatric neurologists were clear in their evaluations that Thalia had a behavioral disorder that placed her on the autism spectrum. Donnie and Lorena took the approach that their response had to be as transformative a moment for Thalia as was hearing the devastating news of her disability diagnosis.

Thalia's journey would have almost certainly turned out differently if Donnie and Lorena had not made an emphatic declaration that they were going to be part of the solution. Their character was tested. Their character was revealed. Donnie and Lorena's acceptance of the situation and their attitude of sacrifice is an example for other parents to emulate. Their sense of purpose never wavered and their hope prevailed. Having thoughts about what might have been is a natural act as one ponders where life is at that very moment. For Donnie, Lorena, and Thalia, the alternative outcomes for their journey can remain just that, thoughts.

ACKNOWLEDGMENTS

THIS PROJECT WAS MOTIVATED BY A DESIRE TO OFFER HOPE to the families that are dealing with the traumatic experience of a child with autism. One way that hope can be conveyed is by people willing to tell their stories. I want to recognize the many others with autism and their families who have written about their experiences. I hope that they find this book is a complement to their efforts and contributes to everyone's understanding of the challenges of autism.

Thalia showed tremendous courage in sharing the details of the most difficult moments in her life. She deserves high praise for her willingness to do so. Donnie and Lorena too had to revisit their toughest days. They overwhelmingly feel that revealing all that is chronicled in this book is well worth it if it helps one family.

Thalia, Donnie, and Lorena were generous with their time through countless interviews and reviewing drafts of the manuscript so that my description of events is accurate. Lisa was interviewed extensively for this project. Lisa recalled her time working with Thalia. Her review of drafts of the manuscript was extremely valuable. Other family members were interviewed. The collective memories of Thalia's grandparents and aunts were instrumental in telling this story.

Much of the rich detail provided in this book is courtesy of the documents that Lorena saved about Thalia's disability. Lorena wrote to the DLC staff on October 3, 2000, one month after Thalia started school, "I wanted to know if I can make copies of Thalia's journal and keep for my own reference." Lorena provided me with two years of daily journals from the DLC, pediatric neurologists' reports, IEP meeting reports, and school report cards. These were the documents that Lorena showed Thalia to help her understand all that she had overcome. These documents which are quoted throughout the book allowed for a more accurate portrayal of Thalia's journey.

Lorena also had a videotape of a therapy session between Lisa and Thalia. Lisa and I watched the videotape of her working with Thalia. Lisa explained how she was trying to develop Thalia's behavior skills. Lisa helped with my knowledge of autism and the applied behavior analysis teaching method. Conversations with Dr. Nicolas Abreu, Assistant Professor of Neurology at the New York University Grossman School of Medicine, and Dr. Jo Ann Delgado at Columbia University's Teachers College assisted with my understanding of autism diagnosis, symptomatic behaviors, and treatment procedures. This book would have been incomplete without their knowledge.

I had valuable assistance aside from the main participants of the story. I received constant encouragement from the faculty and dean's office at Fordham University's Gabelli School of Business, especially my colleagues in the Area of Communication and Media

Management. I am thankful for the support from our administrative assistants, Valerie Mastriocovo and Elizabeth Cardiello. Yukta Murjani is a student in Fordham's undergraduate business honors program. She helped me collect media articles that showed the state of autism diagnosis and treatment at the time when Thalia was first evaluated.

My many faculty mentors and friends are always an inspiration for my work. I am proud that I remain in close contact with my dissertation committee members from when I was a Ph. D. student at the Rutgers University School of Communication: Brent Ruben, Ron Rice, and Shannon Martin. I would like to recognize the faculty from my time as a professor at the University of Texas Department of Advertising and Public Relations. I also continue to always draw great motivation from the students who take my classes.

A conversation with Kevin Mardesich about storytelling was helpful. Kevin is a professor at UCLA. His straightforward explanation about storytelling was posted on my desk as a reminder of what I was trying to accomplish: establish the world, establish the characters, establish the conflict.

Michael Balletti reviewed an early draft. He gave me valuable advice about the organization of the book and the elements of the story that a reader might find the most attractive. The book is simply better because of his contributions. I am grateful.

Finally, it is necessary to provide a brief comment on my involvement in this project. One of Maria Morsillo's older brothers was my grandfather, Luigi La Luna. Lisa and Donnie are my third cousins. To be trusted to write this book and tell Thalia's inspirational story has been an honor of a lifetime.